Phil Pennington is a senior re
worked for RNZ for a decade, mostly producing the
news programmes *Checkpoint* and *Morning Report*.
He helped cover the 2011 Christchurch earthquake,
and in 2008 went to Washington DC to produce RNZ
Morning Report's coverage of the US presidential
election won by Barack Obama. Phil has received a
national media award for feature writing. He has also
worked in newsrooms in Britain and Asia. He and his
family live in Wellington.

SURVIVING

7.8

NEW ZEALANDERS RESPOND TO THE EARTHQUAKES OF NOVEMBER 2016

PHIL PENNINGTON ⦿ RNZ

HarperCollins*Publishers*

HarperCollins*Publishers*

First published in 2017
by HarperCollins*Publishers* (New Zealand) Limited
Unit D1, 63 Apollo Drive, Rosedale, Auckland 0632, New Zealand
harpercollins.co.nz

HarperCollins*Publishers*
Unit D1, 63 Apollo Drive, Rosedale, Auckland 0632, New Zealand
Level 13, 201 Elizabeth Street, Sydney NSW 2000, Australia
A 53, Sector 57, Noida, UP, India
1 London Bridge Street, London, SE1 9GF, United Kingdom
2 Bloor Street East, 20th floor, Toronto, Ontario M4W 1A8, Canada
195 Broadway, New York NY 10007, USA

A catalogue record for this book is available from
the National Library of New Zealand

ISBN 978 1 7755 4110 3 (pbk)
ISBN 978 1 7754 9141 5 (ebook)

Cover design and internal design by Lewis Csizmazia
Cover image by shutterstock.com
Typeset in Times New Roman by Kirby Jones
Printed and bound in Australia by Griffin Press
The papers used by HarperCollins in the manufacture of this book are a natural, recyclable product made from wood grown in sustainable plantation forests. The fibre source and manufacturing processes meet recognised international environmental standards, and carry certification.

Dedicated to the people of the Kaikōura
and Marlborough districts

New Zealand Red Cross 2016 Earthquake Appeal

Within hours of the 7.8 earthquake on November 14, 2016, New Zealand Red Cross established the November 2016 Earthquake Appeal, enabling generous and caring people and organisations from across New Zealand and around the world to support the people affected. Contributions from the sale of this book will go to this appeal, and to support the training and resources of Red Cross Disaster Support and Welfare Teams, so that they are ready to respond to the next disaster in New Zealand, wherever it may be.

Contents

Introduction

'We're rising up — we didn't expect we were going to rise 2 metres, but we're rising up'
— Rob Roche, to RNZ, Nov 30

This book is about the people who survived the Kaikōura earthquake of 2016, the world's second-equal most powerful quake of that year, centred under the dry North Canterbury hills of New Zealand, and one of the most complex earthquakes ever studied by seismologists. The survivors are still recovering.

Just after midnight on November 14, multiple faults ruptured at a speed of 3 kilometres per second. Mountains moved; huge slips plummeted down towards a coast that rose by up to 6 metres. New reefs, 1.5 metres high, now stand exposed where before there was only sea. As if that wasn't enough, the quake also completely cut off the tourist town of Kaikōura.

A thousand tourists needed urgent evacuation, but there was no way in by land for days. Whale-watching boats were stranded at their moorings for weeks, and people's livelihoods disrupted for months on end. The place on which they stand has been changed irrevocably.

I was in the first team sent by public broadcaster RNZ to the heart of the damage zone, just hours after the quake. I experienced the incredible shaking myself at my home in Wellington, and was out on the streets reporting within the hour; that story is told here, too. No buildings fell, but many were damaged and had to be evacuated, and some have since been demolished. In responding, RNZ drew on all its experience, including that of reporting on the Christchurch earthquake of February 2011, which killed 185 people.

The RNZ news teams' reporting of the night of the Kaikōura quake, and the events that followed, has been essential for the public to grasp the magnitude of what has occurred. This has been one of the most significant events to be covered in the history of New Zealand public radio; it was, I believe, the first time that cash-strapped RNZ chartered a helicopter on its own to get its people in — and not just once, but many times.

This book is a distillation of that reporting. At its heart are the people we met and spoke with. I have transcribed interviews with dozens of people who went through the quake; the pictures by RNZ video journalists tell their own story; and I have included social media comments about the events from dozens of others. You may find one of your own tweets here. Jacqueline Pantenier, whom I think lives in Louviers, France, sent this one in response to the story about Mark Solomon and his ruined home: 'Un homme courageux'. That sums up what you are about to read.

Phil Pennington
Wellington
December 2016

1

MONDAY:
THE FIRST FEW HOURS

Is everyone OK? #eqnz

— RNZ, tweet, Nov 14, 12.08am

'I thought the world was coming to an end'

— Julia King, Clarence River, to RNZ, Dec 12

'Yes, Wellington, we are undergoing a fairly dense
earthquake at the moment … this is long and rolling
and getting worse … I can honestly say I doubt I will
be able to stay in the chair for much longer …'

— presenter Vicki McKay, RNZ news bulletin, Nov 14, 12.02am

12.02am —

'… you'll just never believe what has happened'

— Rebekah Kelly, Hurunui, to RNZ

Stealth and power — these are the hallmarks of a major earthquake. It arrives unheralded at the spot on which you stand or the bed in which you lie, and sends you reeling. Your family or friends can be all around you, next to you, clutching you, and you cannot help them; your partner may be on the other side of the bed, your child may be under a table across the room, and in that moment you are powerless to reach them and powerless to stop the shaking and swaying. In those moments, you feel tiny and the forces beneath you massive, even malevolent. You are caught up in a geological rollercoaster ride from which there is no way off and for which there is no stop button. You feel as though you have been king-hit by the very Earth casting aside its moorings. It would be an awe-inspiring thing to go through if it wasn't so damn frightening; if it wasn't so damn unpredictable; if it wasn't so damn unstoppable.

Two minutes and 56 seconds past midnight on November 14, 2016, and RNZ's Vicki McKay, who has been doing the graveyard shift (from midnight to 6am) for longer than the decade I've been around at the radio network, has only just eased herself into the presenter's chair for what she thinks will be another routine night on air, when she is ambushed:

'Yes, Wellington, we are undergoing a fairly dense
earthquake at the moment … this is long and rolling
and getting worse … I can honestly say I doubt I will
be able to stay in the chair for much longer …'

Vicki has to grab the table to stay by the microphone as her
chair rolls around under her. 'My chair moved sideways, but I
was being bounced up and down,' she says. 'I did wonder about
the huge noise coming at me from above, and thought maybe the
ceiling would collapse. I've found out since that it was because
the music library, the biggest in New Zealand, is on the floor
above, directly above me, and the huge cabinets had banged and
crashed into one another.' One listener writes in: 'I don't know
why she didn't run screaming from the studio.'

Instead, Vicki stays glued to that chair for the 2 minutes of the
quake itself, and then for the next 5 hours as the public voice of
a major disaster. RNZ's digital team joins in, doing online what
Vicki is doing on air. Vicki presents the news, and — with Susie
Ferguson — talks to callers, interviews reporters in the field
and seismologists in the studio, relays the latest Civil Defence
warnings, and reads out the tweets and texts as they come in.

@radionz It woke us up in Kaponga, Taranaki. It felt
like a massive train was roaring past the house
— Brad Markham, tweet, 12.10am

@radionz felt in Gore thought I was going mad

— Kim Johnson, tweet, 12.13am

@radionz Moved our house from side to side for
a while in Hamilton

— JNW Ellis, tweet, 12.16am

A swathe of central New Zealand has been jerked from deep sleep to turmoil. Don McIntosh is in bed in his new home in Mt Lyford village, in the hills inland from Kaikōura, when the earthquake hits. 'I honestly thought that we wouldn't make it or that we would come out of here seriously injured,' he says. Stephanie Wang of Texas is in Kaikōura itself, asleep at The Albatross backpacker hostel. 'I was on the top bunk so I thought I was going to die, I thought I was going to fall off the bunk.' Instead, she leaps from the top without using the ladder and flees outside. Anna Barrett is in a central city hotel in Wellington with her husband and daughter. She is from Thailand and has never felt a large quake: 'Oh my gosh, the building is just like swinging, you know.' There is the odd bit of understatement: '@radionz a lil shaken,' tweets Bex Martelletti at 12.10am.

It is without doubt the biggest earthquake I have ever felt. I and my family are shaken from sleep in the Hutt Valley, 2 hours after going to bed with a faint feel of the back-to-regular-work-and-school blues about us. All of us are half-pitched, half-scramble out of bed. My wife and I run for the kids, grab them where three bedroom doors intersect in the bungalow's main hallway, and hold on. At least we can run; at least we can stand. The house yaws and sways. It goes on for what seems to be an age; it appears to be over in a second — both of these hold true when I think back. I can't recall hearing anything at all, but others tell me there was a roaring or crashing or rumbling. I admit to uttering an extreme expletive as I grasped my daughter's shoulders, ducked in the doorway. The kids' eyes are wider than I've ever seen before. Thousands of others are also finding it gut-clenchingly terrifying.

> @radionz big shake here in Rarangi, Blenheim — lots of shelves down and kitchen a mess. Kids frightened, but all well
>
> — Rob Simcic, tweet, 12.31am

> Our chimney thought it would introduce itself to the neighbours #eqnz
>
> — Richard Bicknell, tweet, 12.34am

> And the terrifying sound … #eqnz
>
> — Code Club Aotearoa, tweet, 2.22am

The power is out. After pulling some clothes out of the wardrobe, the first thing I grab in the dark is my phone, to get the size of the quake off GeoNet and look for a tsunami warning. We huddle in the kitchen. I can't remember the kids saying anything. Perhaps they are too terrified to speak? We can't decide whether to evacuate or stay. Surely you can't simply go back to bed after something like that? (Surprisingly, though, as everyone shares their 'quake story' in the days to come, rolling back over and going to sleep is an option some went with, especially the 20-somethings.) In our house we are split: I say go, my wife says stay, arguing that it wasn't so big that we fell over so maybe we don't need to evacuate. We keep checking and rechecking, but can find no tsunami alert. The consensus — spurred by my teenage son who hasn't been up so early since he hit puberty — is edging towards staying put and not evacuating.

My next call is to the newsroom to tell them I'm coming in to help out. I know others will be doing the same — not just reporters, but also emergency workers and hospital nurses and doctors, and contractors and police and power-lines people. I know that the more hands on deck at times like this, the better. Crucially, I can see that our house is undamaged and none of us is in tears or appears too shaken-up. We are all possibly a little too shocked for that, although this only occurs to me later. Many things only occur to me later — like the wisdom of abandoning my family when, really, we have no idea exactly what is going on. I'm sure it's like this for tens of thousands of other people at this same moment, and was like this after the Canterbury quakes in 2010 and 2011. You make your decision. You hope by God it's the right one. My family and I agree that if a tsunami alert comes through they'll drive up the hill suburb of Maungaraki, or walk, as the road up is only 400 metres away. I head off, feeling a little guilty and very unsure.

———

Biggest shake I've ever felt in #Wellington. Absolutely terrifying. Frayed nerves being calmed by 'Ardijah' — thank you @radionz #eqnz

— Lorenz Wright, tweet, 12.31am

Vicki McKay would never normally play music at a time like this 'because people are so unnerved'. (Ardijah is an Auckland R&B band.) But it buys her time to move to a bigger studio with a second microphone for Susie Ferguson. RNZ goes to rolling coverage. There is a skeleton crew of six people in the newsroom, including news director Mary Wilson who'd been at her desk all evening and was still there at midnight as usual and who helps orchestrate what follows. They get back out from under their desks and scramble to make sense of what is going on even as their own nerves are jangling loud enough, it feels, to almost block out the rising tide of ringing phones as the public calls in, desperate to know more. The team cannot fill dead air with bad information that risks alarming people without good reason, but getting solid information is hugely difficult. GeoNet and its sensors provide the bare numbers: 1 minute and 1 second after the quake hits, it is recorded as a magnitude 6.5 on the Richter scale and 25 kilometres deep, centred near Cheviot; another minute later and it has been upgraded to a 7.5. A duty seismologist is quickly on hand, and on air. But calls to Civil Defence hit the obstacle of time — it's maybe 20 minutes before first responders get into the national emergency centre in a bunker under the Beehive. Reporting the news also runs into the obstacle of damage — calls to the Kaikōura area are failing as multiple cell-towers have been damaged and not all landlines are working. The major fibre-optic cable that runs down the east coast of the South Island, and that supports both cell and landlines, has been severed in at least six places, putting all the load on to the west coast cable. Updates are flashed online, and producer Lucy Hall hammers the phones, dashing into the studio with bits of paper bearing the latest updates, aware that, first and foremost, people want to know whether they need to evacuate in the face of an incoming wave:

> 'Please be aware that there is no tsunami warning —
> and this is terribly important, terribly important — that
> there is no tsunami warning at this stage and Civil
> Defence, we are in touch with them ...'
> — Vicki McKay, on RNZ, 12.41am

Morning Report presenter Susie Ferguson checks on her kids and then speeds in from home, noticing all the broken glass in the streets. 'I was on the phone to the office within 30 seconds of the shaking stopping, so in retrospect the RNZ building on The Terrace was probably still bouncing — it's a really bouncy building,' Susie says. 'I spoke to our bulletins editor, and she was in so much shock she couldn't even speak to me ... When I arrived, I said to Kim Griggs, the *Morning Report* deputy editor, "What can I do?" ... She just looked at me and said, "Get in the studio." And that's how it all began. I just got in there, put my headphones on, and Vicki and I started talking to each other.'

The pressure is on: 'RNZ.co.nz is under heavy load right now, but we're live blogging,' the digital team tweets at 12.44am Kim Griggs had been putting the finishing touches to Monday's *Morning Report* programme, but immediately scraps it all. 'It was an absolutely terrifying 120 seconds, but when the shaking stopped, we dusted ourselves off and then our rolling coverage began,' says Kim. '… Lucy and I started putting more and more people on air — officials, people texting in, reporters and other RNZ people as they bravely went out to see what was happening.'

In the midst of it all, Vicki is acutely aware of avoiding the flare of panic:

> 'I know it's not a laughing matter, but we are not trying to be too dramatic about it at this stage, because that only puts fear and panic into people, and quite frankly, we need our wits about us … so if a little bit of levity can be injected when things are tough, we're going to go with that, because it worked last time and it certainly can work now …'
> — Vicki McKay, on RNZ, 12.41am

___

Cascading dominoes

> '… just glass, glass, glass everywhere and we just ran out in bare feet'
> — Steve Dale, Mt Lyford, to RNZ

The Earth has ruptured. At some yet-to-be-pinpointed spot in North Canterbury the incredible tension between two tectonic plates has given way, sending cascading dominoes of pressure south and especially north up a whole series of fault-lines, within seconds hitting Hanmer Springs, Waiau and Mt Lyford, then yammering up the seaward side of the main range to hit Kaikōura 17 seconds later, then on up the coast through Clarence, Kēkerengū, Ward and Seddon another 13 seconds on. It is an unstoppable wave, triggering landslides, lifting coastlines, moving mountains, wrecking houses. People tell RNZ reporters what they went through:

> *'When it hit, I ran outside. We've got a pond, it's about 18 metres in diameter ... The water was going up in the air about 2 metres with the light of the [supermoon] on it. I could just see it blowing, and I called to my wife and son to just get out — I kept yelling, "Out, out, out."*
>
> *'And everything was just coming off. We've got big glass lamp shades, they were swinging 2 metres and smashing into the sides of the roof and just coming down on us, all the drawers were coming out — just glass, glass, glass everywhere, and we just ran out in bare feet.'*
> — Steve Dale, Mt Lyford, to RNZ

On the Kaikōura Peninsula, Noel and Denise Collingwood, barefoot and barely clothed, hot-foot it out of their South Bay home up to a road above. 'I was in bed, my wife was just coming to bed and then everything just started crashing around,' Noel says. 'So we … went to the pantry to try to get the keys, and what supplies we had in there, but everything was scattered all over the floor. I cut me feet on the glass. So we gave that a miss, went out in the garage with the car keys, couldn't get in the garage, so we had to scarper up the hill. And I was only in me boxers and a T-shirt and it was dark — couldn't see where we were going.' Denise has cracked two ribs because the dresser drawers fell out and hit her in the chest. 'She slipped on where the subsidence was on the track on the way up and did more damage,' says Noel.

Stephanie Wang from Texas is staying with friends at The Albatross backpacker hostel near the seafront in Kaikōura. 'I was asleep because I was meant to go on a dolphin swim the next morning … I was on the top bunk so I thought I was going to die, I thought I was going to fall off the bunk. Didn't even try to find the ladder to climb off — I just jumped off. I've just never been in an earthquake … so I was pretty frightened.'

Victoria Greenwood-Loose, in the Marlborough coastal settlement of Rarangi, experiences a gentle rumble — then the quake hits with tremendous force. 'We've always been told [that] if it goes longer than 2 minutes then you just get out. It was so strong that we just had to run — and we did.' She, her partner and five-year-old son and 20-month-old daughter make it downstairs and up a hill.

A motel manager in Ward, David La Grice, is sleeping in a house-truck when his partner, Jules, and eight-year-old son, Lachie, come running from the house, yelling. Together on the lawn, they hear their immediate neighbours start to call out to one another. 'So we yelled to people up and down the road. People were starting to come out of their houses — probably about six of us for about half an hour, yelling out, "Are you all right?", not knowing what to do next,' David says. They head for the school, but then stop, trying to work out where the higher ground is. 'So we thought, "Why don't we just go up to the motel and we'll set up a bit of a thing out the front?" We ripped all of the mattresses out of the motel and put them down, and put a whole lot of the older people under gazebos with blankets, and put a whole lot of mattresses down for the kids, and just kept boiling water. Some guy turned up with a barbecue, so everyone was eating pork chops at two o'clock in the morning.' People keep trickling in as word gets around, and in the end about 80 people are camped out in front of the A1 Ward Motel.

A horde of crayfish make a run for it at the Burkhart fish factory in Ward when the bins topple over in the holding room. 'There were crayfish crawling everywhere,' says Kerry Snell. 'I think it was 2 tonnes of crayfish, just all crawling around. Disoriented, too, as we all were.'

——

There are stories of people screaming, crying, yelling, being frozen to the spot; of terrified children doing the exact right thing and taking cover, of other children sleeping through it; of people holding each other, holding the furniture, holding it together. There's a lot of laughter — a lot of it nervous, and some of it wry — often accompanied by an understated assessment of how someone's most precious financial asset has probably had it. A man in Alicetown, Lower Hutt dashes straight into the street amid the shaking, only to realise once it stops that he has no clothes on since he doesn't wear pyjamas. Later, I hear about a girl from Germany who was in Christchurch for the February 2011 earthquake and is now in Kaikōura and thinks she's kind of jinxing New Zealand. I hear about the Murray household above the Clarence River, where 40 people flee to high ground: 'We all ended up here and lit a bonfire under the tree, and all got some chairs and rocked her out,' says James Murray.

I get to the RNZ office on The Terrace in Wellington at 12.25am. The motorway from Petone into Wellington is undamaged, though I'm a little leery driving over the flyover above Aotea Quay and have to remind myself that it's been quake-strengthened. Through my mind flash images of collapsed highway flyovers in California after its various big quakes. I forget to check the big illuminated road signs for a tsunami warning, but later see photos of the alerts shining in the dark. On the city streets, scores of people are huddled on footpaths at corners and traffic lights, many staring up at the multi-storey buildings they've just fled from. I drive six floors up the ramps in the parking building RNZ uses — if I'd stopped to think, I'd never have ventured inside; who knows what buildings have been compromised? In the office, I ask whether we know about any casualties yet, or where the worst damage in Wellington might be. The answer is no, it's too soon for that. I grab a small workbag with a Nagra audio-recorder, microphone and spare batteries in it, and head out. I'm not frightened, though I am a little nervous — how will I make sense of what is out there when I have so little back-up information? It feels like going out into the void. I forget to take a hard hat.

Outside, sirens are sounding everywhere and a strong wind is blowing. I head across the road to people milling around the doors of the Atrium building and begin interviewing them, then move along to outside the James Cook Hotel, doing the same. Having a task to do helps settle my nerves; I guess this is how emergency workers feel, and perhaps why they regularly appear so calm. Heading down Boulcott Street, I come across three young people carrying emergency supplies they've rushed out with from of a student hostel; fortunately, all the students had left on their summer break just days before. I do my first live-cross to Vicki:

> 'So I'm walking up the top end of Lambton Quay. I can see a fire truck coming towards me very, very slowly. I've come down from The Terrace … there are hundreds of people in the street, people are standing around looking fairly dazed. I have seen a little bit of damage, there's some glass on the pavement … that's fallen it looks like from one of the hostels … I talked to people standing outside the James Cook Hotel …

one of them, she reported that there was some
damage on a skywalk up above and she was reluctant
to use it, and so didn't come down that way, and
others spoke of all of the doors in the passage being
flung open and some damage inside the rooms ... I'm
just walking up the bottom of Willis Street now; I have
heard that there's some damage further up here. You
might be able to hear as I go, there's a fair few alarms
ringing, and there's a sort of klaxon sounding further
up on the hill, which is a sound I've not heard before,
so it's all fairly disconcerting. And another fire truck is
going past me just as we speak, and that's heading
north up Willis Street, so I might just turn around and
start to follow it ...'

— Phil Pennington, to RNZ, 12.45am

Such is the shaking that at 1am the atomic clock RNZ relies on
for the sound pips at the top of the hour is knocked off its game.
Instead of the pips, the news is introduced with one long, low-
pitched hum that lasts until a technician pulls the plug. The hum
itself becomes part of the rolling coverage:

'RNZ news at 1. Good morning, I'm Vicki McKay. We
apologise for the feedback that you are receiving
at the moment, um, we have a technical problem
of some significance and we are attempting to fix
that ... [the feedback hum stops] It has been fixed;
my apologies ... The police say the emergency

111 line is not working as aftershocks continue around the country … after a massive shake just after midnight centred on Canterbury.'

———

In the dark

@radionz Police in Kaikōura door knocking to get people to move up hill

— Ina Kinkski, tweet, Nov 14, 2.19am

@radionz family members in waiau had to travel a fair distance to inform us they were okay. The little town is a mess and bridge collapsed

— Beka Elizabeth, tweet, 4.23am

While I and other reporters are in the streets of Wellington in the small hours of Monday morning, my RNZ colleague Conan Young is driving through the dark from his home in Christchurch, aiming for the quake's epicentre in North Canterbury. He has no idea what he will find. He recalls the events:

We're both woken sharply from our sleep by the shaking at our home in Christchurch. Where once we would have taken a few seconds to comprehend what is happening, after years of aftershocks we know straight away what this means. I head to my daughter's room, my wife to my

son's. My six-year-old daughter knows what the shaking means as well, and has already adopted the turtle pose all children here have now had drummed into them: head down and hands over her head to protect it from anything that might fall.

I keep waiting for the swaying of our 100-year-old bungalow to switch to something more violent, but it never moves out of first gear, the lamp shade swaying back and forth but nothing being knocked off shelves. That's when I realise: it's somebody else's turn this time.

After what seems like an eternity, the rumbling stops. It's the middle of the night, but as I cycle the short distance in to work, I notice people standing on street corners and lights on in homes. I won't be the only one not getting a full night's sleep this evening.

As I drive north, I call some friends living just a block from the beach in South Brighton to warn them of the tsunami alert. The sirens on their street haven't sounded, but they've already moved inland. My first stop is Amberley, where a welfare centre has been set up at a community centre for those along the coast who don't have anywhere to evacuate to. The sirens haven't sounded here either; that job has been left to the volunteer fire brigade members who've driven around the handful of coastal settlements here urging residents to leave.

Initial reports talk about an earthquake centred near Hanmer, and Kaikōura being cut off. By the time I get to Waipara, State Highway 1 heading north has already been closed. The man at the checkpoint says the road's not too bad but they don't want anybody using the bridges until they've been checked by engineers, something that won't be possible until it gets light. I'm told I can still use State Highway 7 to Hanmer Springs, and decide to try for Kaikōura using the inland route, via Waiau and Mt Lyford.

My way is blocked again just outside Waiau by another 'Road closed' sign. I ask a contractor if I can walk from here. He lets me past with a reminder to be careful. It's still pitch dark and I can only see a short way in front of me, thanks to my head torch, but it doesn't take long before I come across a huge slip where a cliff has given way and sent debris and rocks spewing across the road. Then I look down and see cracks in the chip seal stretching for 10 metres in front of me. I quickly decide it's time to leave, and make it back to the road-block in time to feel my first decent aftershock rumble up through the ground. I'm glad I'm not close to that landslide.'

——

'BREAKING NEWS — Tsunami warning issued for all southern coastal areas of New Zealand'

— RNZ, headline, Nov 14, 1.08am

> What does Southern coast mean???? On Kapiti coast
> ... do we move??
>
> — Sarah Main, Facebook, 1.08am

Conan is in the dark in North Canterbury. He can only feel his way forward, hoping for the best, hoping he can make it. It's a feeling shared by many throughout New Zealand. Information on what is going on and what to do is like the light of a torch — narrow and jerky, and extending such a short way into the night that it only emphasises the blackness beyond. Jamie Milne on Facebook at 1.20am asks of the tsunami alert: 'What about the southern coast of Wellington?' Julie Howard in the Christchurch suburb of South Brighton says her elderly relatives are door-knocking in the dark and alerting their elderly neighbours and families. 'This is just bloody appalling communication on the ground,' she messages RNZ's Facebook page. The GNS duty seismologist is on air within minutes, telling people to take the tsunami warning seriously given the water-level change measured around Kaikōura, and this is tweeted by RNZ at 1.20am.

I still have no idea about the tsunami warning. Disasters expose your oversights, and one of mine is that I haven't brought with me a second cellphone to listen in to what's happening on air, for real-time warnings and updates. At about this time I am passing in front of the central library in Wellington and notice bits of broken masonry on the footpath. I have done a loop up lower Willis Street — which is quiet and appears undamaged, the jutting-out fantastic glass façade of the new Spark building intact as far as I can see from the glow of the streetlights — then across into Victoria Street. Outside the library I look up but can't see any cracks. Still, I step out from under the arches of the covered walkway, onto the street. I carry on, heading north now. There are no cars, I see no people.

I know that Featherston Street buildings suffered some significant superficial damage in the August 2013 quake centred on Seddon, so I head there. Once again, windows and glass awnings have showered pebbles of safety glass into the street in numerous places. Water is pouring down the face of one building and splashing around the parking meters. I see cracks showing between an office block and an old building with a pub on the ground floor. A large rusted gutter has fallen off Agriculture House. A lone man is crossing Waring Taylor Street; he tells me he's just been checking on everyone in their rooms at the nearby hotel where he's staying. I hear a large bang behind us and suddenly feel vulnerable, realising that I have no hard hat. I can't see what's fallen, so press on northwards, towards Parliament and the railway station, knowing that one particular building down here, the near-new BNZ building on the wharf, shook loose its ceiling tiles in 2013. I want to see how it has fared.

A clutch of shift workers are outside the main door of New Zealand Post's headquarters on Waterloo Quay. They tell me there's not much damage inside, but felt it was wise to get out. Backpackers huddle, some in blankets, on the steps of a hostel a few doors down, opposite the main railway station. The doors to the station are shut, which is usual at this time of night. But glass has fallen out of the bus shelter roofs and is scattered on the ground. I ask a taxi-driver waiting in the rank, as if he is going to get a fare — on this of all nights — if he has seen any damage around town, but he looks startled and uncomprehending.

Sirens continue to wail all across the city. At the BNZ building opposite the railway station, the alarm is interspersed with an instruction along the lines of 'Evacuate the building, please use the fire exits'. The sliding glass doors are wide open into the lobby, which is awash with broken safety glass, and the next set of sliders into the courtyard is also wide open. Ray, a driver for Huttons, is parked up in his truck out front, on the phone to a workmate who, like him, is wondering what to do. 'I'm meant to do deliveries, but I'm not going in there,' he tells me, gesturing at the glass-strewn lobby. The glass-façade building is only a few years old, but it lost a lot of ceiling panels in the 2013 quake; this looks worse. Ray tells me he's heard that roads are wrecked and the port's badly damaged, but doesn't know exactly where.

I leave the BNZ, heading for CentrePort. A car with 'Harbourmaster' on the side pulls up, and a grey-haired man tells me that the link-span they attach to the back of the ferry for loading vehicles on has fallen down. He's trying to find out more details himself. I head down that way, past Westpac Stadium, where the footpath is rucked-up like a fold in a duvet and one panel of the big iron-railed fence guarding the port along Aotea Quay has fallen down. I cross over to take a photo of it on my phone. The odd car goes past, but very few. I stop and call in to the studio, and do a short live-cross to tell them about the BNZ and what little I've learned about the ferry terminal. But it's hellishly windy and, although I have ducked behind a lamp-post and am trying to shield the phone, the distortion is too great on air, so we ring off quickly.

> @radionz why the hell is a reporter in the street in the
> middle of aftershocks. Stay inside! #eqnz
> — Dagan, tweet, 1.13am

At the Interislander ferry terminal it's hard to tell, in the dark, at a distance, what damage has been done to, or caused by, the fallen link-span. One end appears to rest on the wharf. A worker tells me it wasn't the shaking that knocked it down, but that the ferry pulled away suddenly from the wharf, heading for the open harbour in case of a tsunami. The Interislander manager who emerges from the office isn't inclined to let me, or the AFP stringer who's turned up, get any closer to take pictures of the link-span, or tell us just what's going on. That is, until he gets word from Civil Defence that everyone needs to get to higher ground straight away, so he tells us to leave, too, as they bundle into cars. I call the newsroom. They want me to head to the hills above Kilbirnie where they've heard evacuees are gathering, and send another reporter, Kate Gudsell, down in a car to get me.

News of the earthquake is rolling around the world like a wave. Expat New Zealanders are alerted by news flashes and scrolling headlines: 'Strong earthquake shakes New Zealand,' says the *New York Times*; 'Deadly earthquake strikes New Zealand,' says Al Jazeera; 'New Zealand hit by aftershocks after severe earthquake,' says the BBC. CNN, Reuters, ABC — headlines on these and other websites, relayed and amplified on social media — trigger a deluge of cellphone calls, Facebook messages, texts and tweets.

> From two worried kiwis in London, thank you for your updates
> — Emily Simpson, Facebook, 1.31am

> Listening in from Melbourne
> — Sapphire Khalid, Facebook, 1.39am

> There's a neurotic kiwi in NYC right now, relaying info to family in 3 parts of NZ, thanks to yr reporting
> — Lydia Nobbs, tweet, 4.38am

The tsunami alert is being broadcast on air and online. Mass evacuations are unusual and, in Wellington, we expect to see a lot of people on the move. But we don't. Kate Gudsell picks me up at the ferry terminal and we head for Kilbirnie and the airport and the hills above Miramar. We know that another reporter is on her way to another high point, Mt Victoria, where we've heard people are gathering. The streets are still largely empty of cars. There are no streams of apartment-dwellers on the footpaths fleeing the lower ground. However, the tweets show that some people are obviously out and about, watching the coast.

@radionz sea dropped super low at Lyall bay then
filled up fast but nothing over the walls

— Simon Morton, tweet, 1.25am

'BREAKING NEWS — Tsunami warning, following
severe quake, has been extended to the eastern coast
of the North Island'

— RNZ, headline, 1.31am

Oh dear god. @radionz having to tell people to not
go sightseeing. Smh [Shaking my head]. People who
need to be told …

— Prance MacCarol, tweet, 1.56am

There is ongoing confusion and uncertainty. 'There's no tsunami sirens going off in Christchurch. I'm not sure what to do … my wife and son are both fast asleep,' Danny Goulter messages to the RNZ Facebook page at 1.54am. Kirsten Knight asks whether Tawa is 'safe from the tidal wave'. Connor Smith is in limbo: 'We don't know what to do in Dunedin, we are waiting for alarms to go off,' he writes at 2.06am. In Christchurch, RNZ reporter Katy Gossett heads up Scarborough Hill above Sumner and calls into the studio to go on air with Susie Ferguson:

Katy Gosset: 'We could see a few people parked up in cars, you know a few sort of wide-eyed-looking kids sitting in the backs of cars in puffer jackets, but not a heap of them. And what's happened in the last 10 minutes or so is that the sirens started, probably just after 2, about 10 past 2, and that has really prompted action. So I'm standing at the moment on the top of Scarborough Hill and I can see quite considerably more activity down in Sumner — lights are on ...'

Susie Ferguson: 'It seems almost strange that we've been talking about the tsunami warning that's been issued for some time now, but only now that the sirens are going off.'

Katy: 'It does seem odd and indeed we do, in Sumner, have practices for the tsunami sirens from time to time, so you know, we're aware of them, we know what they sound like — but we haven't heard them until, as I say, 10 minutes, quarter of an hour ago ...'

— RNZ, 2.20am

'BREAKING NEWS — Severe earthquake that hit NZ early this morning revised up from magnitude 6.6 to 7.5'

— RNZ, headline, 2.25am

Everyone here is sleeping clothed tonight — if we sleep

— Steph, tweet, 2.25am

Meanwhile, Kate Gudsell and I are on our way to Kilbirnie. We see glass scattered in front of a new apartment block outside the national museum, Te Papa. We stop, and a middle-aged man comes out. He's a little drunk, but tells us the glass has fallen from a deck balustrade above. He's been checking on the little old ladies who live in the apartments. 'We're okay,' he says. We head off, and the studio calls, wanting a live-cross. I do it from the passenger seat of the car as we round the bends of Evans Bay. It's at this time I learn, from Vicki McKay, that the tsunami sirens have gone off in the Hutt Valley where I live.

Phil Pennington: 'Vicki, I'm in a car travelling around Oriental Parade heading for Lyall Bay, and I must say, having heard what you just said about the evacuation order for all people in low-lying areas of Wellington, we're not seeing that on the ground. We are the only car on the road — we've probably seen two or three other cars coming the other way, but that's it. Most cars are parked up — it seems to me that most people have been shaken up and they've gone back to bed. There are a few houses with their lights on, but we're certainly not seeing signs of any sort of mass evacuation.'

Vicki McKay: 'Now, Phil, we've just had a report in that you'll be interested in: tsunami sirens are going off in Lower Hutt at the moment. So I would imagine that anyone on the foreshore at Petone or Eastbourne should evacuate to higher ground.'

Phil: 'Yeah, I actually have something to say on that 'cos my family are from Petone. I'm very thankful to know that they are up in Maungaraki.'

— RNZ, 2.40am

Any news on the Hutt please?

— Elisha Johnson, Facebook, 2.41am

@radionz sirens going here in Lower Hutt north of Hutt Hospital. Cars all over the road. We are staying put on your advice

— Henry Clayton, tweet, 2.54am

Vicki tells us she's received a text saying the hills above Seatoun are full of cars. 'So perhaps people have already moved, those who were going to,' she says. One of the main roads up these hills winds up above Peter Jackson's movie base in Miramar to the disused Mt Crawford Prison. The road turns into a corridor of cars from about halfway up; people are parked left and right, filling a reserve and off up into the night. Most people shelter in their cars, their faces reflecting the glow of screens. Some stand around, comparing notes; one or two have only their pyjamas on. A family in front of us has just climbed out of their car and the parents are wrapping a rug around a young boy. It's windy and cold. They tell me they're on their second evacuation, and they're not the only ones — they came up, wondered whether they should have bothered, went back home, and then heard the Civil Defence warning. The woman works at the airport, and she's worried that some of her colleagues may still be working there, though it's after two in the morning.

Further on I meet Howard Cook, who tells me they heard the warning on the way back from Hataitai where they'd driven to check that his wife's shop was okay. 'My son had a bag packed, ready to go, so we headed up the hill. We thought we'd come up [the main road] and there's been just thousands of cars coming past. When we got up here there was probably half a dozen cars, but since then it's been non-stop.

'We were umming and aahing about coming up after the initial quake,' Howard says. 'But … then the proper warnings came through so we thought, "Bugger it, we'll come up the hill."

'At the house [it] was quite funny when the earthquake happened: I grabbed my wife and put her under the door, which I know is not the right thing to do, but it was the closest thing — and I had one hand around my wife and one hand holding my TV.' He laughs. 'Yeah, I know what my priorities are, my wife and my TV.' Is the TV all right? 'Yeah, the TV's fine.' Is the wife all right? 'She's all right, yeah. She was in tears though before, yeah, yeah, 'cos it wouldn't stop, it just wouldn't stop — well, you felt it, it just wouldn't stop.'

At least one household invites people in to use the toilet. Nelma Pierce and Jill Cameron, who are neighbours on the flat, drive up after hearing the warnings. 'That's when it becomes real and you get quite scared,' Nelma tells Kate. A young family is crammed in a car, and the mother gets out to talk to me. She says the grandparents arrived on the Sunday from India, but this is a good thing because at least they are together, rather than being apart and worried. I recall when the September 2010 quake hit Canterbury, my family and I were staying in a caravan in Cornwall and had no idea it had happened until our British holiday-neighbours hurried over with the news. They knew we were New Zealanders and genuinely wanted to know if we were all right. It was touching.

In other parts of the coast around New Zealand, people are also evacuating. At Te Awanga, in Hawke's Bay, locals gather at Haumoana School, freaking out at the possibility of a big wave. 'We are concerned about our home and everything that's there, but our lives are more important,' says one. 'I just went to the kids and said, "It's an emergency, we have to go — get a sweatshirt, grab some shoes, we have to go."' From the Far North to Mangawhai, sirens sound, and Northlanders who call 111 are told to evacuate immediately. A short time later, RNZ runs the headline: 'QUAKE LATEST — Civil Defence in Canterbury is evacuating its entire coast area over the tsunami threat.'

> Would really like to know how long I have to sit on a
> hill in Dunedin, in a carpark full of people, with my cat
> — Vickie Cross, Facebook, 2.56am

One place in Wellington that is *not* evacuating is the international airport. We park outside the terminal on our way down from the hill road, heading for the office. It's just after 3am, and for quite some time Civil Defence has been telling everyone in low-lying parts of the region to evacuate. But the airport is open. The prospect of a tsunami coming directly from Cook Strait, over the seawall and straight down the runway doesn't seem to faze them. I ask three men in high-viz jackets walking past the Wendy's counter inside the terminal about why it is still open. They won't say, telling me to call the airport's PR person on the phone, so I leave it.

Australian tourist Tony Barrett is coming out of the airport men's room. He hasn't mucked about: despite having bad legs and hips, he's got his wife, Anna, and her daughter down the stairs at their central Wellington hotel and they've come straight to the airport. They've swapped a swaying hotel for a low-lying airport, but they feel safer now. 'I thought that I was dreaming or something,' says Anna Barrett, 'and then the bed was shaking so I woke up, I ran out and then I tried to get my daughter. I said, "Earthquake!" She said, "No, I'm sleeping, I'm sleeping." I said, "Get up — earthquake! Get out from the hotel." Oh my gosh, the building is just like swinging, you know.'

There are scatterings of other people, waiting, dozing. The first domestic flight out, to Nelson, is good to go at around 5am. I imagine that things might not seem so normal if these people were standing on the runway facing south over the breakwater, staring out to sea and wondering what was out there off the Kaikōura coast in the dark.

Out at sea, hundreds of people are stuck on Cook Strait ferries. One of them, Tim Bennett, is in his car down below, ready to get off in Picton, when he hears a lot of rattling and clanking. He assumes it's the preparations for docking. 'We were in the hull in our vehicles, and they hadn't dropped the back door down yet when it happened. So if we were minutes earlier we would have been in the process of unloading, which would have been a different story. And they came over the loudspeaker and said they had had an earthquake and they were just going to go back out.'

> @radionz Tim stuck on the Interislander — anchored just off Picton — unable to disembark. No power in Picton so stuck on the ferry #eqnz
> — Kerrie, tweet, 4.13am

RNZ's Nelson regional reporter, Tracy Neal, detours to Picton in the dark when police cordons block her way to Seddon. 'There was just too much damage to bridges to get across,' she says. 'But it was very eerie being near the coast ... All the sirens were blaring at Montana Wineries, it was a very eerie moment ... I spoke to some young Picton chaps waiting for family to come off the ferry, and they had witnessed the strange light flare that sometimes occurs, ... as a precursor to very big earthquakes, ... and these chaps saw it and they said it looked like a UFO, just bright green and blue lights and then it hit.'

> Just heard on RNZ a scientist debunking the 'blue'
> flashes in the sky ... We saw this happening here in
> the Wairarapa and it sure was not a figment of our
> imagination.
>
> — Yvonne Baylis, Facebook

Back in the RNZ newsroom, more and more people have been arriving, picking up what needs to be done in order of urgency. *Morning Report*'s Kim Griggs is still here, and producer Lucy Hall — calm, unruffled — is calling people who are texting in to see whether they will go on air. 'When Gerry Brownlee was about to go live from the Beehive bunker at about 4:30am, we had to jury-rig a way to get that on air,' says Kim. 'So we tested Skype with the reporter in the bunker, Chris Bramwell, who gave us a minute or so's warning. We Skyped her, she held her phone up to the minister and we crossed our fingers the line would work. It did.'

> 'QUAKE LATEST — Reports of casualties in the
> Kaikōura area, but nature and extent not yet known —
> Gerry Brownlee'
>
> — RNZ, headline, 4.49am

'That we knew what to do is because we already had the template of RNZ's unrivalled rolling coverage during the Christchurch quakes,' says Kim. 'By 5am a new team came in to continue the rolling coverage and to start sending even more reporters fanning out around the quake-ravaged parts of New Zealand.' A friend of Kim's writes in from Hamilton: 'I thought, "Good, Kim's on, we'll soon be hearing what is happening with all this scary-as-shit shaking." And we did.'

Kate Gudsell and I get back to the office as dawn breaks, and spend the next two hours cutting interview audio to get it on air. The country is hearing what people have been going through. However, it's only now — after a whip-around of what's being reported from north Canterbury, Kaikōura, Marlborough and elsewhere in Wellington — that I, along with people all around the country, begin to grasp the extent of the impact. There is still uncertainty about the most pressing question, that of casualties.

'Earthquake: New Zealanders in shock. Authorities are scrambling to assess damage and respond to reports of injuries after the severe earthquake, which shook much of the country after midnight'
— RNZ, Facebook, 5.50am

We are telling the small stories within the disaster while trying to grasp the whole picture, rather like a jigsaw puzzle where you hold only a few pieces in your hand. A post from Theresa Mazur on RNZ's Facebook site at about this time captures the uncertainty. She has a daughter, grandson, granddaughter and son-in-law in Christchurch, whom she last heard from at 10.22pm on Sunday. 'I wait to hear news that all is well,' Theresa writes.

'Quite a few residents in the centre of Wellington out on the streets, in their pyjamas, pretty shaken, pretty upset … I met a girl out in the street … she was still a bit too shocked to go back inside. I asked if I could go up and have a look. She'd said it was a bit of a mess, fish tank exploded … Yeah, I didn't feel unsafe until I went inside that building, to be honest: a lot of cracks, a lot of plaster, a lot of water.'

— RNZ video journalist Rebekah Parsons-King, on *Morning Report*, 6.19am

Oops, slept peacefully through the whole event and I'm only metres from the waters edge … until this am, ignorance was bliss!

— Rosemary Halso, Facebook, 6.51am

On RNZ, *Morning Report* is going to air. They need me to go back out to report from the streets in the slot after the 7am news bulletin. I take my workbag and go out once more. I don't have much time, so I do a quick figure-of-eight up Willis, down Featherston, onto Lambton Quay, and past Parliament and the courts. As the day lightens, the disorientation of the first few hours in the dark after the quake is receding, and I feel a lot less vulnerable. It's just as patchy, though, trying to determine what's happened. At the Bank Arcade, a man is unloading a big water vacuum from a van. The building's maintenance man tells me that sprinkler pipes on the second floor cracked in the shaking, flooding the floors and stairways, down through the Starbucks on the ground floor and the Lush soap shop and other upmarket stores at the basement level. A clutch of men in high-viz vests gathers outside Victoria University's multi-storey law faculty building fronting the all-wood Old Government Buildings opposite the Beehive. They say only that inspections of the just-renovated university building are under way. I end up back at the damaged BNZ building on the wharf, and report:

'I'm actually down at the wharf … There's some pretty serious-looking cracks in the wharf as it runs around to where the containers are kept … I don't know how serious that is, but in the 200 metres or so that I've covered there's at least three sets of zig-zagging cracks. As I've walked through town, Lambton Quay and … Featherston Street, got a series of buildings showing some signs of damage: we've got some cracking on the exteriors of buildings … The buses are running, there's a couple of shops that are open … but very, very quiet here, and the railway station is closed … It's more like a bit of a ghost town at the moment'

— Phil Pennington, on *Morning Report*, 7.44am

Phil Pennington: 'On Featherston Street, in a space of 200 metres, we had [structural engineers] walking along — one coming one way, one coming the other — looking for cracks, broken windows, that type of thing … We had two police at an intersection, we had a truck that's putting down cones to redirect

the traffic, and a man sweeping up what he said
was only 10 windows that had broken this time on
his building — in the 2013 quake he had a hundred
windows that had broken, so he was quite happy …'

Kim Hill: 'You don't wear a hard hat, do you,
Phil? I haven't seen you with a hard hat on.'

Phil: 'I have one at home, and next time I'll be
bringing it.'

— Phil Pennington, on *Morning Report*, 8.38am

It is not until just after 9am that we are able to responsibly report on the death toll from the quake. 'On the best information we have, there have been two fatalities,' RNZ says at 9.04am. Thirty-three minutes later, we are able to firm that up: 'QUAKE LATEST: Civil Defence confirm two people killed in earthquake.'

Behind the headlines is the tragedy for those two families. But the death toll is amazingly low given how much the earth has moved. The confirmation is, as it turns out, somewhat premature: even a day or two later, the authorities will have failed to make comprehensive checks on people by air. I hear from several groups gathered in isolated spots accessible only by helicopter, such as farms above the Clarence River and others along the Kaikōura to Cheviot road — no one has stopped to check on them. Clarence farmer James Murray lets rip about this. However, I can picture him also shaking his head in disbelieving gratitude when, later, he reflects on what could have happened on State Highway 1:

> 'It was just so lucky that this earthquake was at 12 o'clock at night. If this was the middle of the afternoon on Sunday or even 10 o'clock on Sunday night, the thousands and thousands of people that would've [been] killed on that road would have been unbelievable. Like, you know, that road was pumping, my son came back from Christchurch that day, on that Sunday, and he got back about six o'clock and he said it was 80 kays all the way from Christchurch, it was bumper-to-bumper. So it was just luck when the earthquake hit … It was dark and it was scary, but if it had been in daylight the deaths would have been huge.'
>
> — James Murray, Clarence, to RNZ

2

MONDAY: KAIKŌURA BY AIR, AND MT LYFORD

'Thieves have ransacked the home of a Christchurch family who had temporarily evacuated their house following the earthquake'

— RNZ, Facebook, Nov 4, 11.10am

'Quake recovery efforts will be hampered by the weather today, with severe gales expected to hit the upper South Island and lower North Island'

— RNZ, Facebook, 12.10pm

The logger and the ute

'How are you going to get around? ... You can have
my ute.'

— Bob Dronfield, Kaikōura Airport, to RNZ reporters, Nov 14

Monday, 11am

Central New Zealand has taken a king hit, the second-equal largest earthquake by magnitude worldwide in 2016. It reverberated out from under the dry hills of North Canterbury, up the saw-toothed Kaikōura ranges and down, down under the sea into Kaikōura Canyon and the Hikurangi Channel, carrying shudders up to Gisborne and beyond. In its wake, people are dazed and scared. For hundreds of thousands of us throughout central New Zealand, nothing will be normal about the next 24 hours. An earthquake like this exposes our vulnerabilities — and even in a disaster, there are thieves poised to prey upon property. They quickly set about doing just that. But for every rotten apple, there are 10,000 who are sound — people who are shaking themselves off, clearing their heads, looking around and setting to work.

Eleven hours after the quake, our chopper is flying over Clarence where we see the first real damage closer to the quake's epicentre. The helicopter flight has been a close-run thing to organise. RNZ digital editor Alex van Wel was on the phone from 5am trying to get space on a flight in with another media organisation, but no go. The options are narrowing as more helicopters are called in for emergency operations. At 8am, though, we get the green light for a 10.30am take-off from Kapiti, with reporter Tim Graham, video journalist Bex Parsons-King and myself on board.

There's been no time to go home and grab a bag. No toothbrush, no change of clothes. In the dark that followed the power cut, I'd grabbed whatever came to hand from the wardrobe. Now I realise I have a hole the size of a 50 cent coin in the backside of my trousers. My green trainers have holes in the toes. But we have a first aid kit, some water and snacks, and the gear we need to record sound and pictures and, hopefully, get it out from a disaster zone where the state of communications is a truly wild card.

We pass over Cook Strait and above the creased hills of Marlborough — from this height, it looks like any other day. But at Clarence our pilot, Jeremy Mitchell, has cause to swoop in closer. The centre-line of State Highway 1 south of the Clarence River bridge does not match up anymore. At the crux of the fault, the white-painted road markings on the south side are perhaps 2 or 3 metres to the west of the markings on the north side. There is a concertina of cracks from one verge to the other on either side of the split. As we watch, a four-wheel-drive approaches from the south, drives off the tarseal and down into the uneven trench on the side — and makes it past. Twelve hours before, this was a 100 kph zone.

A little further south we see a red-and-white Cessna parked in a layby beside the highway, next to a farm ute or two and a couple of cars. We land in a paddock to check it out. Jeremy grabs a quick word with one or two locals over the fence, but time is ticking by quickly and we have to get back in the air if we're to be over Kaikōura by midday. Jeremy tells us that the pilot's flown up from Southland to check on his family.

From this point on, the scale of the damage begins to become apparent. The highway is fractured in numerous places. Slips the height of skyscrapers fan out hundreds of metres across the highway and the railway line. Tim voices up a piece while Bex shoots video, in the hope of being able to send this through to the newsroom when we land:

> 'We're in the air, and from up here the scale of the damage is very dramatic. Fallen trees, huge slips covering chunks of State Highway 1 on the coastal road north of Kaikōura … and some of these slips have actually pushed the railway line out to the sea as they have gone. That is clearly going to take months and months to fix.'
>
> — Tim Graham, to mic in the helicopter, 11.55am

A few minutes later, the cliffs and bluffs give way to the flat land of the river mouth at Hapuku, and we see Kaikōura itself up ahead, the beach sweeping to the left of its dramatic peninsula. The amount of damage to the road and railway line that we've seen from the air on the way down is in striking contrast to the picture of seeming normality below us here. We can't see a single flattened house or damaged building. The fields are green and bright. The sea is as it ever was. But even from a thousand feet up, the place does appear oddly still. There are no cars on the highway, and hardly any on the streets in town. A timberyard's chimney is not pumping out any smoke. We see no tractors working in the paddocks, or boats out off the peninsula. We're scooting forward at a rate of knots over a town whose vibrancy has been a magnet for tourists for going on 30 years, but it looks like a snapshot, a postcard below us: frozen.

Although we can't see any damage, we know that the Elms Homestead, an historic local farmhouse, has been flattened and one person has died there, so we need to attempt a flyover of it. At this point it strikes me that in the rush we've forgotten to bring a map. Aerial photos of the homestead have appeared online, but we have no idea exactly where it is, and the pilot doesn't either. We have to give up on that. We'd counted on having cellphone coverage right above town — but there is none. There's no way of doing the scheduled live report by phone from the air for the top of RNZ's *Midday Report*, which begins with a 15-minute news bulletin and continues to 1pm. We had been going to make the call in the air, then swing west immediately to get as far towards Hanmer Springs as the aircraft's fuel and time would allow, in the face of what Jeremy says is an incoming front and his need to get back home. Now we have to land. We have to find a phone that works and get on the radio as fast as we can. We are out of time — Kaikōura, as we're about to discover, is out of a lot more than that.

'The noise of the sea, it was roaring'

— Bob Dronfield, to RNZ, Nov 14, 12.20pm

We land at Kaikōura Airport. I don't know what I had expected:
an aerodrome with an asphalt parking lot for one, and a handy
Avis office. This has neither. RNZ boss Paul Thompson had told
us to hire a car — or 'borrow one', he said. We won't be hiring
here. There's just a mown landing strip next to a tarseal one,
and two buildings. State Highway 1 runs right alongside, but it's
empty of anything to flag down. I run to the first building, Tim
at my heels. Wings Over Whales is deserted, its large windows
broken into dangerous shards. Briefly I consider — then dismiss
— trying to jump in through the broken glass to find a phone to
call the radio. Time is ticking by; it must be a quarter past midday
by now. The second building houses the aero club; it's locked.

A ute pulls into the gravel parking lot — the sign on the door
reads Dronfield Logging. Bob Dronfield gets out, and I yell across
to him. He's expecting a chopper to fly him out to his home in
Amberley, but sure, he'll run us into town 5 kilometres or so away,
and back. On the way, he tells us about the night he's just had.

'Jumped out the window of the house 'cos I couldn't get the door
open,' says Bob. 'The noise of the sea, it was roaring, an incredible
noise, right through the earthquake. I don't know what causes
it … It wasn't waves, it was just like an underground noise just
coming up from the sea … but the sea was flat as.' He didn't muck
about. 'Got in my ute and drove to the top of the hill — pronto.'

Bob laughs, and points ahead through the windshield. 'Stopped and saw a couple of neighbours on the way and we just followed each other up the road here, right here just behind the racecourse.'

We're coming up on the racecourse at the turn into South Bay and the bottom of the hill that leads up to the main part of town. The road up has crumbled like cake in two places, where it is down to one lane. I remember someone at RNZ getting through to Kaikōura mayor Winston Gray on his cellphone at just this spot in the early hours of today. And sure enough, Tim's got a signal at last. We pull over at the racecourse, and Tim does our first live-cross, into *Midday Report*, from the passenger seat of the Dronfield Logging ute:

> 'The landlines have been knocked out, so talking to you from the racecourse here. And the drive to the racecourse was a pretty rocky one, entrances and exits from bridges pretty buckled, and the road kind of undulating in some parts … We actually did see a plane that had landed on a section of State Highway 1, because the road is obviously closed and the pilot was not sure whether he would be able to land at an airfield.'
>
> — Tim Graham, live-cross to RNZ *Midday Report*, Nov 14, 12.45pm

The live-cross done, now it's all about making the best use of the chopper waiting for us back at the airport. From what Bob Dronfield tells us, we need to get to Mt Lyford and Waiau, up the Inland Road. At this early stage, he might be just about the most informed person about what's destined to become one of the defining stories of the quake: the fractured state of the Inland Road and the desperate attempts to open up this lifeline to the town. Bob's already driven up there this Monday morning, and it's not a pretty sight. He tells us that the road is riven by multiple deep cracks and there are lots of slips. He's had to drive slowly, his empty truck-bed bouncing. He kept pushing on, but at 17 kilometres or so, that was it: he could get no further. He tells us this while driving us back to the airport. We pass it on to the RNZ producers in Wellington and Auckland. The grapevine is at work.

'How are you going to get around?' Bob asks, as the airfield comes into sight. We admit that we don't know. 'You can have my ute,' he says. Just like that. Maybe it's the Kiwi thing to do — as is Tim's response along the lines of 'that won't be necessary', which thankfully Bob doesn't hear. We arrange to leave the keys somewhere for him to pick up when next he's back. The only thing he asks is that we make sure no one nicks the two cubes in the back seat; the blue and green plastic Warehouse boxes are stuffed with $7000 worth of health and safety planning material.

The ute still has two-thirds of a tank of diesel in it. We have no inkling of how precious this is going to become over the next few days. It's only much later, while on the phone from Wellington to Bob's wife, Michelle, in Amberley, that I learn that the quake has thrown their whole logging business into jeopardy. All their heavy machinery is trapped in a forestry block, and it could be weeks — or months — before the road is cleared. Bob has said nothing of this. I ask Michelle how they'll survive. 'I don't know,' she says quietly.

—

The homestead and the hero

> '"It's utter devastation." The PM, acting Civil Defence minister and Opposition leader are travelling to some of the areas worst hit by the 7.5 magnitude quake …'
> — RNZ, Facebook, Nov 14, 4.40pm

> 'That's a goodie.'
> — a pilot on the PM's chopper commenting as an aftershock hits, sending more rockfalls down and dust skywards

Monday, 1pm

We are back on the chopper, aiming to retrace the trip Bob Dronfield made by ute and continue on from where he had to turn back. Once again racing the clock — and mapless — we're startled to see below, almost immediately after we lift off, the wreckage of the Elms Homestead. It turns out it is just a few hundred metres across the highway from the airfield, hidden by some trees. We're unable to do more than bank around as Bex shoots some video and I record:

'This is it. It's completely collapsed as you can
see, the iron is simply sitting on the walls that have
collapsed outward. There's masonry, bricks, rubble
everywhere.'

— Phil Pennington, to mic in the chopper, 12.50pm

Louis Edgar, 74, died in the homestead, and his 100-year-old mother, Margaret, was trapped under a collapsed double door. Father-of-five Dr Chris Henry was on duty when the quake hit — he got to the homestead and, alongside a firefighter, crawled through a window to find Margaret. Chris had won a bravery medal during the 2011 Christchurch quake, as one of three rescuers who crawled on their bellies through the collapsed CTV building to reach trapped students. Here he was doing the same thing again.

'It was a kind of surreal moment,' Chris tells RNZ shortly after the rescue. 'I was thinking, "This is really strange here" … especially going to a collapsed house thinking, "I know what this is like, and this isn't easy to deal with." Driving down the road, these crevasses had appeared. It was reminiscent of Christchurch, there was a very odd sense of *déjà vu* about the whole thing.'

Initially, it seems impossible that anyone could have survived. 'The house looked so bad … The fire brigade did a careful and quiet check of the whole place. We found there was someone still alive in the rubble. There was so much broken glass, and she had bad feet. We basically just carried her and shuffled out. She told me to be careful and not to cut myself, which was ironic. She was very together, really. It took quite a while, she would have been stuck in there for 2 hours maybe.'

Louis Edgar's wife, Pam, was also rescued. Chris Henry doesn't want to talk to media about it much. He's the quintessential self-effacing New Zealand hero. Like anyone else whose story appears here, he'd be embarrassed to be described as one. But that's how it is with heroes: it's only others who get to nominate them. Chris wants the focus to be on responding to the ongoing needs of the district, not on him. But, in a sense, talking about the heroism of doing what's necessary when the earth is moving, as he did, *does* meet an ongoing need — the need to lift people's spirits, the need for inspiration, perhaps the need to give everyone an 'I-could-do-that-too' moment.

Heroism takes many different forms. In Kaikōura town, Rob Roche dispenses with all but the rudiments of sleep to immediately set about making a huge difference to hygiene and sanitation — his crews carry out rubbish and portable-toilet deliveries day and night. Meantime, Rob's fairly new home on Mount Fyffe Road, 4 kilometres outside town, has a 1-metre-wide, half-metre-deep trench under its foundations, and he has no idea whether or not it is a write-off. Even though Rob and his family are homeless, there's work to do, so they roll their sleeves up and get on with it. There's also a bloke who simply calls himself Pete; he's the hermit of Rakautara, a tiny settlement near Ohau Point where eight people are trapped for days. A wee chap,

Pete skips nimbly across the face of a dangerous slip to complete the final 100 metres of pipe connections needed to get water to the cut-off houses. 'We didn't want him to do it,' Rakautara local Tahua Solomon says of Pete, 'but he insisted, and he got the pipe across.'

———

The lodge owner's refuge

'… the community from Mt Lyford started to come down to meet here as a meeting place, as a place of refuge really. So that's how it went down.'
— Jenny Yeoman, Mt Lyford Lodge, to RNZ

'Yeah, nah, it's just phenomenal to what it could have been.'
— Kevin Keehan, to RNZ, Nov 14

Monday, 1.10pm

Our helicopter wheels away from Elms Homestead, heading southwest up the valley, in the lee of the Seaward Kaikōura Range. It's an impressive landscape, with a lot going on in a small space — beach, coast, valley, farmland, river, foothills, and mountains high enough to still have snow on them in mid-November. The old State Highway 70, the Inland Road, winds along below us; occasionally it's possible to see the thin, dark lines of cracks across it, sometimes there's a series of them a little like the lines on a seismograph. There is zero traffic, and no sign of any farm work going on in the surrounding bright green fields.

Jeremy alerts us to a faint cloud of dust to our right, rising up behind an improbably steep ridge, and he swings us over to take a look. By the time we get there, the last of the dirt and rocks in this landslide are tumbling hundreds of metres down into a V-shaped gully where the creek is already thoroughly blocked up. It's the first of several puffs of landslide dust that we see over the next 2 hours as we make our way up towards Waiau and back. Similar landslides are blocking the Ote Makura Stream above Goose Bay — and, with the water backing up behind the impromptu dam, Civil Defence orders an urgent evacuation of 30 or so households in the bay on the afternoon of November 23.

'QUAKE LATEST — Slip dam risk triggers evacuation of 35 homes in Goose Bay near Kaikōura'
— RNZ, headline, Nov 23, 3.54pm

We follow the grey poles of the main power-lines that feed Kaikōura, expecting to see breaks along the way. We don't, though in places the poles are leaning over. The road below becomes worse, the slips across it occurring at ever more regular intervals. We don't have enough fuel or time to make it to Hanmer or even Waiau, so it becomes a guessing game of when to turn back. We pass over a substantial log-cabin-style building and spot a ute with a trailer on the back heading towards it, making slow but steady progress over a tortuous bit of damaged road, so we opt to wheel around and follow it back to the log cabin.

Jeremy sets us down in a layby, 300 metres from the building. We walk up the middle of the highway with zero chance of being run over. Normally it's a 55-minute drive from Kaikōura to Mt Lyford Lodge, and 20 minutes from Waiau township. Not today. The road here is a tortured mess of ruptured tarseal running for 200 metres before it dead-ends in a slip that, by the day's standards, is of merely medium size; it still covers both lanes and spills down the far bank above the river. I stand in the deepest crack in the road, which reaches to my mid-thigh. The pattern on the tarseal is one we will see again and again — cracks running along and across it, many thin but some wide, that have opened up as it has been stretched apart and then has slumped sideways during the shaking. It's very much like the effect you get when you stand on top of a low sand bank at the edge of an estuary and push down with your toes until the sand begins to give and crumble. And we all know what happens if you push a bit more. Where it has cracked, the tarseal layer looks as thin as cake icing. We turn and walk back towards the lodge, down the middle of the highway, pine forest on one side, river on the other.

The 20-kilometre-long winding hill road between Mt Lyford township and Mt Lyford Lodge is open, but both town and lodge are entirely cut off from Waiau to the southwest and Kaikōura to the northeast. The ute and trailer we were tracking from above is nowhere to be seen, but as we come around a wide bend we see the two-storey lodge: it's big, brown, solid and substantial, reassuringly so for the 30-odd people of the village who came down in the early hours to take refuge here, lighting a campfire out the back for comfort. One woman in the village died; all we know at this stage is that it was of a medical condition as she ran from her home. Understandably, no one at the lodge wants to talk to us about that.

Lodge co-owner Jenny Yeoman, 63, and another grey-haired woman are standing outside, under the massive eaves. I walk up and, before I can stop myself, the words — inane even to my ears — are out of my mouth: 'How are you?' Jenny's stare is a dressing-down in itself, befitting a retired teacher of several decades' experience. 'Can I ask you some questions?' I hurry on. 'Not if they're dumb ones like that,' says Jenny. The double-doors to the lodge are open, and the sound of broken glass being swept up comes from inside; Jenny makes no move to show us in. Her stance is protective of her lodge, as if she'd prefer that I didn't go in. 'Sorry, that sounds so rude, doesn't it?' she says of her rebuff. I assure her that today of all days, it doesn't. And she goes on to tell us her story.

'Well, overnight, about midnight, our whole building shook hugely at the top.' She gestures to the second floor. 'My sister and brother-in-law were up there and I was up there, and we actually managed to get out after furniture and stuff tumbled on us. Got downstairs to where my parents are staying with us at the moment. And really, we just held on.' She takes a ragged breath.

'And the community from Mt Lyford started to come down to meet here as a meeting place, as a place of refuge really. So that's how it went down.'

Jenny is from the North Island, and notes that it's South Islanders who know all about quakes. She is clearly leaning on that, on their experience, at a time when — just five months after buying the lodge as a retirement project — she already has more than enough going on. 'We got it up and running and ready to really steam ahead, and now this … Not good, not good.'

They have no cellphone coverage, no internet, no landlines. 'So, nothing.' People from the village have stayed to clean up, to cook meals. 'We are actually working as a community for the good of everybody,' says Jenny. As if to punctuate this, there's a particularly loud crash of glass from the kitchen. 'At the moment this is a base for people to be safe.'

—

It becomes apparent very early on that Mt Lyford, Waiau, Kaikōura and the region to the north are physically cut off for people who lack a chopper or a boat. The slips covering State Highway 1 below the Clarence River have brought down thousands of tonnes of rubble, which spews out to the new high-tide mark of the raised rocks of the shore. No one can get past other giant slips to the south, towards Goose Bay and Oaro on the main road. We've just seen from our chopper the ructions along the Inland Road.

'So the slips here are horrendous … and you've got to believe it's in the billions of dollars to resolve these issues, they're huge slips … I'm not sure how long it will actually take to move this level of rubble off the road, not to mention the damage to the railways.'

— John Key, to RNZ, Nov 14

'New Zealand quake: The cut-off tourist town of Kaikōura'

— BBC News, headline

The district's communication links are hugely compromised, with uncertain landline links and many cellphone towers damaged so that mobiles work only part of the time; we find it's easier to call Wellington or Auckland than to phone someone within Kaikōura. We have no email. Wi-fi comes and goes depending on where you are. People are outside the hospital in town day and night trying, and often failing and trying again, to get through to family, friends, social media and news websites.

No one wants to be an experiment, a guinea pig, but there's an element of Kaikōura being in a test-tube. How many times have so many people been so drastically cut off in this way, anywhere in the world — or at least in the First World? And yet, how many places in New Zealand are vulnerable to just such disconnection on their own ribbon of coast squeezed in between the mountains or high hills and the sea? Think of the West Coast, Gisborne, New Plymouth, Wellington. The Canterbury quakes tested emergency responses in one way and the Kaikōura quake in another, exquisitely relevant to anyone living on a strip of land that could be ruptured at either end. Kaikōura — so compact, so contained and so vibrant, with its strong Māori history and connectedness to the land, its abundant sealife, and its 740 businesses in a district of 3500 people — now becomes a tough but fascinating study in resilience that applies to all New Zealanders.

The damage in Kaikōura spreads across power, water, sewerage, roads and communications, each layer having been cut through shockingly abruptly. There are still further layers to being cut off, like a nest of Russian matryoshka dolls: the town and district of 3500 people is cut off from the region; within this, the 30 or so families in Mt Lyford are cut off by slips in either direction on the Inland Road; zeroing in again, individual families are cut off from their neighbours.

One such family is the Lidgards, just south of Ohau Point. It takes 11 days before a chopper flies in to get them out. With their own power source, a working sewerage system and a nearby creek, the family of four make it through reasonably comfortably — plus they have icing on their cake: 'We've got internet up there — we were watching movies on Netflix in the middle of a disaster,' Annemarie Lidgard tells RNZ. 'It was quite surreal.' The most brutal disconnect, though, is leaving. 'As we grabbed our last bags and I walked down to where the chopper had landed, I had tears in my eyes,' she says. 'You just don't know when you'll be back.' Or even *if* you will be back.

Aftershock

Another aftershock. 6.6. #eqnz

— Mark Gilbert, tweet, Nov 14, 1.40pm

'You're lucky I didn't swear'

— Jenny Yeoman, to RNZ

We're still at Mt Lyford Lodge, where Jenny Yeoman is holding it together along with those who've come down during the night from Mt Lyford village. One, Doug Simpson, brings a trailer with a big container of water on it; someone else brings a small generator which hums out the back of the lodge as I talk to Jenny. 'We have supplies in the kitchen that we're going to make freely available, and we're going to make do with what we can. All pull together,' she says.

'[We] lost a lot of precious things, personal things … total wipeout of our kitchen and bar facilities. However,' her voice catches, 'we didn't lose a life … and no one's hurt, no one, not one person … I'm very surprised, because the way this building was shaking and the noise, I expected something really horrific, especially with my 85-year-old parents down the bottom, and no, everybody's fine.'

I ask if they are completely cut off. 'Apparently. Apparently we can't go very far up that road,' she points towards Kaikōura, 'and apparently we can't go down there further than Waiau, so yes, we are, we're stranded in a way.' I begin to tell her it's worse than that, that the road's impassable well before Waiau.

But then we feel it, Jenny, Bex who's been videoing the interview, and me. For me, there's a fraction of eerie silence when my subconscious realises what's in store and the adrenaline kicks in, before the physical quake accelerates up through the balls of my feet and the bottom plates of the building, through my body and up the walls, and finally on up and out, rattling the roof. It's sickening to experience — an aftershock that's a shuddering whump. We all start backwards, wincing, on the hair-line between ducking and running, or dropping. Then it's over. Jenny, Bex and I stand straighter, and psychologically shake ourselves down. There are nervous chuckles. The recorder is still running; 'You're lucky I didn't swear,' Jenny says. GeoNet records it as a magnitude 6.3, 35 kilometres deep, centred just north of Cheviot, though someone tweets that it was 6.6. It was one of a little flurry of four large aftershocks around 1.30pm.

I ask if this has been going on all day — and was that the worst of them? 'All day, since 12 o'clock last night, it's absolutely relentless,' she says. 'The one before was worse … 3 or 4 minutes ago, you were up in the air … but this is pretty much how it's going.'

I fear my final question might get a similar response to my first, but I ask it anyway: can she carry on? Jenny casts a steely eye over me, and lists the tests of her mettle: she's been a primary teacher, school principal and lecturer, and has worked overseas. 'So this is a new venture. I'm retired, and I learned to pull a beer and make good coffee, so yeah, that's my dream, you know, to have an adventure running a business with my sister and her husband.' Will she make it through? 'Absolutely,' — said with double the steel — 'absolutely. We're going to be open again … It still stands. We will be on the road. Don't ask me when, but we will keep going.'

———

In a hole

'The ruptures are clean breaks and are often hard to spot until you're right on top of them. Road crews haven't been up here yet to lay out road cones and warning signs.'
— Conan Young, Nov 14

Early in the afternoon on Monday, near Wellington, RNZ presenter Vicki McKay is waking up at home after snatching some sleep following a long night. She's in for a surprise. 'It's ridiculous,' says Vicki. 'I got a message from someone saying, "You've gone global, you're on the Huffington Post, the BBC." … I woke after that shift, and I hadn't got much sleep, the funniest thing was my daughter saying, "Mum, you're famous, you're all over social media. They've recorded you when you were on air, and it's on social media." I cracked up, of course. I was just doing my job. What else was I going to do?'

'Huge fissures in the road, the road has given way in many places. I lost count of [the] times we had to slow down and drive through a paddock to then get back onto the road again. At one stage we actually missed a 1-metre drop, went straight into it, had to get a local farmer to bring his tractor down and pull us out of this huge hole. It's going to be a massive job, even just getting this road open on a temporary basis.'

— Conan Young, on RNZ

Down in Canterbury, RNZ reporter Conan Young has also woken from a hurried sleep after being stymied in his first attempt to get through to Waiau and Mt Lyford. In the dark, he got partway to Hanmer before a contractor pulled him over, telling him it wasn't safe to go any further and to turn back. Now he has a chance to try again, in daylight. Conan picks up the story:

I finally make it in to Waiau, via a back road that removes the need to cross the main bridge into town. I head for the school, where a welfare centre has been set up. It is the township's second day without power or water. As many as 15 homes may need to be demolished because the earthquake has made them too unstable to re-enter. I'm told that even if their homes still appear safe, most locals don't want to sleep in them as they're still terrified of what might happen if there's another big shake.

For now people are sleeping at the school, on mattresses on the floor, or in their cars which they've parked on the playing fields. Volunteers are putting on breakfast, lunch and dinner using food donated by nearby towns such as Culverden, and using barbecues to cook. There are lots of hugs and the mood is light, but I can tell that not many people here have had much sleep. I overhear volunteer firefighter Peter Bush making plans to deliver food to Mt Lyford, where Jo-Anne Mackinnon died from what are thought to be medical complications. She was one of two people to lose their lives on Sunday night.

I later hear a prediction that half of the homes in Mt Lyford, population 23, may be write-offs. Peter agrees to me tagging along, and I help him load food onto his ute from the freezer at the small supermarket in town. No power means that the food needs to be eaten before it defrosts. Peter is glad to get out of Waiau for a few hours, to help 'clear his head'. Between them, he and his wife, Alix, who is the Civil Defence coordinator, have been flat-tack helping look after everybody else and are now starting to feel it.

The inland route to Mt Lyford is badly damaged and, technically, closed. Peter hasn't been up this way since the shake. We pick our way gingerly, having to go off-road when we come across chasms in the asphalt over a metre deep where the earth has given way. In some places long stretches have slid away down hills, like a cake that's collapsed in the oven, and there's no off-road option available. Here you can only inch along the damaged road and hope that what's left of the chip seal remains intact.

The ruptures are clean breaks and are often hard to spot until you're right on top of them. Road crews haven't been up here yet to lay out road cones and warning signs. Peter misjudges the depth of one large dip and bottoms out, nose-first into the hole. We're stuck. We try to get ourselves out, Peter putting weight on the back of the ute and me placing it in reverse, but it's hopeless. He heads down the road to ask a farmer to get us out with his tractor. While he's gone, a Mt Lyford resident, Steve Dale, who's heading in the same direction taking food up to the village, stops to lend a hand.

The strops he ties to our ute break, and we agree that this is definitely a job for the farmer's tractor. While we wait, I ask him how he's coping. 'My wife, she's got cut legs; yeah, so it was pretty hard. Yeah, she's been smashed up pretty bad, um, I got out okay.' Steve's son put his head under the covers during the shaking and pretended it wasn't happening, but eventually followed his dad's instructions to get out. 'I'm just glad I'm okay and my son and wife are okay.' Steve turns away, holding back tears and taking a moment to collect himself. 'We lost everything inside, but that's replaceable, and there's a bit of damage outside, but we're okay. I'm okay about it; you've just got to keep going, you can't stop, can you, just keep going. We've just been told there could be another big one in a couple of days. The Geo guys are saying that. So what do you do? Go and get your tent out of your house.'

I ask Steve about Gary Morton and his partner, Jo-Anne Mackinnon. 'They were trying to get out of their house. She was right behind him, and he just got to the door and he turned around and she'd passed away behind him. They took him out in a helicopter yesterday to Christchurch. He lost his house, it's gone.'

The tractor arrives and hauls us out of the hole. The journey from Waiau to Mt Lyford normally takes about 20 minutes, but today it's taken Peter and me 2 hours. Dropping off the food at the lodge, which is now doubling as a welfare centre, we head a few kilometres back the way we've already come to check on Peter's in-laws. Their house has pulled through, but their neighbour, Don McIntosh, who's now staying with them, hasn't been so lucky.

Don agrees to show me his newly built home, just up the hill, a log-cabin-type construction. 'Even the bed, the bolts that hold all the bed together, were ripped out from the headboard, which collapsed the bed on one side and we were stuck,' Don, a grey-bearded maybe-60-something, says. 'We couldn't get out; we just couldn't move. The movement in the house and the noise was just so bad, you just couldn't move, you just had to wait until it actually stopped before you could do anything.

'It was terrifying, absolutely terrifying,' he says. 'It was going up and down, going sideways, it was rolling, the whole house was twisting and flexing and the noise was just horrendous ... I honestly thought that we wouldn't make it or that we would come out of here seriously injured. As you can see from the devastation, how we both, me and my partner, got out of here without a scratch I just find it hard to believe.'

Don is standing inside his home. His cast-iron log-burner has been shunted across the floor. 'It was lying face forward with all of the ash on the carpet, and we're very lucky we didn't have a fire because it [still had] some hot embers in it from the night before.' Linings have been ripped from walls. The cars in his twin garage have rocked back and forth on their wheels and left two huge dents in the roller doors. A huge boulder in his front garden, a metre high and just as wide, has somehow toppled over. Three 2-metre-high windows in a bay arrangement lie cracked and twisted on the grass outside. Every other window has blown out and shattered, and the house has been shunted off its foundations.

The wind is whistling through. This was Don's dream home that he had hoped to retire in. 'I'm absolutely gutted

... Colin, a friend, is a builder — he actually did a lot of the building on the house — and he said as far as he can see it's totalled. Get our stuff out, what we can get out of it, and it will be just a digger job, pull it to bits.'

———

The fireman and the trail bike

'... you run into a big slip that's on the road and I can't get through it on a dirt bike'
— Hugh Wells, to RNZ, Nov 14, 1.50pm

Down at Mt Lyford Lodge on Monday afternoon, I have no idea that Conan will make it in to the village just a short distance — but a hellish drive — up the road. We haven't the time to push on, so decide that we must head back to Kaikōura once we've recorded a few more interviews here. I walk around the outside path behind the lodge to where a small blue generator is humming in a large gravel parking lot. Next to the handful of parked cars is a large grass camping area. It shouldn't seem odd that there are one or two small tents pitched here, but after the night's events it does. Naturally, it's not a case of tenting holidays going on as usual — instead, the Barnes family pitched their tent here in the dark hours of the post-quake dawn. Claudene Barnes is here with her husband because their 13-year-old daughter is too freaked out to go inside a building.

'My daughter is very stressed, and that's really why we are here,' she tells Tim Graham. 'We've been up since the earthquake hit, and at the moment stress levels are too high for her to do anything else anymore … We will try and have a sleep here … both me and my husband are quite level-headed and can handle that, but she is struggling with that, you know, she's quite a bit younger … We'll pick up the pieces and keep going, no problem at all.' Then she adds: 'I hope I never have that experience again,' and laughs.

Jade Rolph from Cambridge, England, also has her tent set up here. She's six weeks into a cycling tour. 'We're just going to wait and see — we're hoping either the roads will be clear and we can cycle out back towards Christchurch, or we can find a nice local to give us a lift in one of their four-by-fours or something.'

Fireman Hugh Wells, in his high-viz emergency overalls, is chatting with another bloke in the car park. 'If they can all camp down here it'll be good; they can keep an eye on each other,' he says. A trail bike rests on its stand. Hugh has ridden it the 20 kilometres to the lodge from Waiau, where he lives and works as a handyman. 'We've had a few minor injuries, some cuts and things like that, a couple of the houses have been substantially damaged, and a few of the brick houses have had bricks fall off, sort of falling off the wall. We're very lucky we haven't had any more injuries, very lucky.' Another fire-crew mate of his has gone on further, another 5 kilometres down the valley towards Kaikōura to check how things are at Whalesback Station.

'We've actually ridden dirt bikes up to assess the road, to see if we can get people [there] out, and the viability of the road.' Hugh shakes his head. 'At the moment it's not … We've got two bridges that are probably foot-traffic only, the road has got tremendous amounts of drops, cracks. You know, there's anything up to a 2-foot drop, and then there'll be a hole you could park a bike into two or three times and not even see it, so there's a huge amount of repair work to be done to get vehicles up this way, even just four-wheel-drive vehicles … It's cut off. I got as far as I could — it's probably another 5 kays up the road and you run into a big slip that's on the road, and I can't get through it on a dirt bike. I got through one rocky slip … but I can't get through the next one.

'The bridges are all moved and twisted … I didn't look under any of them, so I don't know, structurally, what they're like, but if they've moved there's some problems with them. Well, somebody has to check them out for us, somebody who knows what they're looking at. So hopefully they'll get some engineers in here in the next day or so or tomorrow, hopefully, and check these bridges.'

Only Hugh's fire service radio is working, not his cellphone, so he has limited contact with his family in Waiau. The pressure continues over the coming days. It's made worse when a thief steals the Waiau Volunteer Fire Brigade's main portable pump, lifting it off the back of the truck that was parked at Dog Creek. They'd been using it to fill up to nine water-tankers at a time, to supply isolated properties in the area. Hugh's being polite when he describes the theft as 'a bit rude'. Similarly, when all of the

Kēkerengū Voluntary Rural Fire Force's six radios are stolen by someone who climbs in the community centre window, rural fire chief John Philipson calls it 'a bit low'. He'd been using the radios on the night of the quake as he raced around making sure that people were evacuating. The theft is discovered when a local fire officer arrives to mow the lawns at the centre. Also, just north of Hapuku, a KiwiRail freight train abandoned on the slip-hit line is looted. Three men are later arrested and charged, after turning themselves in. The train itself isn't moved until mid-December.

Small communities are feeling vulnerable. What Murray Campbell of Goose Bay describes as the looting of an evacuated house in nearby Oaro puts him on edge, and ups the ante when his own township is evacuated on November 23 due to the threat from the landslide dam upstream. He heads back in to Goose Bay once or twice a day to feed his animals, and tells me how on one occasion he chased two groups of people out of town. 'We don't know who they are,' he says. 'They might be casing the place.'

Murray and the Mahonys, who lease the motor camp, say police and Civil Defence promised them cordons to keep non-locals out, but what checkpoints there are on the road to Christchurch are very slack. On December 1, the day that 12 of the 17 Goose Bay households, including the Campbells and Mahonys, are allowed back into their homes, Civil Defence apologises about a misunderstanding over the cordons: what it had really meant was that police would be patrolling regularly. That didn't happen either, says Murray. It seems that nowhere is immune —

burglars waste no time in ripping off eight evacuated homes and businesses in Christchurch on the day of the quake.

———

The builder and the seals

'I don't think he ever dreamed that 30 years later we'd all still be doing it'
— Vanessa Chambers, co-owner of Sea Swim Kaikōura

As we make to leave Mt Lyford Lodge in our helicopter, 300 metres up the road, another silver chopper descends and lands on the road directly outside. You can fly, you can trail-bike, you can walk, or you can take to the riverbed in your high-clearance four-wheel-drive, but you can forget about cars and regular transportation. In a standard supermarket-style SUV, you wouldn't get beyond the narrow radius of passable roads around Kaikōura. The hill farms on the Inland Road have become Bear Grylls territory. Cars won't cut it, and I've never seen so few of them on the road. In town, it's like a Sunday afternoon used to be when, as bach owner Keith Beardsley told RNZ's Katy Gosset, 'You could shoot a rifle down the main street … and you were lucky if you hit a seagull, let alone a person.'

Quiet, yes — but the place has always had its attractions, those the tourist industry cottoned on to. They were there before, and remain there now. Mark Boomer of Christchurch has been going to Kaikōura since he was a student, surfing, diving and frequenting the pie-warmer at the old pub. These days he keeps a fishing boat called *Confidence* at his bach. He tells Katy Gosset he inherited the name from a previous owner and chose not to change it. 'It's a good boat. We go 5, 6, 7 kilometres off-shore looking for blue cod, groper and the odd bluenose, so it's good fun.'

Back in the early 1980s, there were 30,000 visitors a year rather than the 900,000 now; well, not actually now, but pre-quake. Almost a million tourists a year in a town of 2000, with another 1500 in the surrounding district. Vanessa Chambers, co-owner of Seal Swim Kaikōura, tells Katy about how her builder dad, Graeme Chambers, helped kick it all off by taking the few backpackers there were back in the day up Mount Fyffe in his Land Rover for a barbecue and the sunset.

The visitors would ask him how he spent his time. So he showed them, spearfishing off the peninsula. The local seals, as ever, pestered them — that is, until Graeme realised that the animals were the real drawcard for the tourists. 'Back in the day,' says Vanessa, 'seals didn't have a very high regard with locals … It was actually the tourists' interest and response to the seals in the water that made Dad realise that people really enjoyed it.'

In 2002, Vanessa and her brother Matthew took over the business. Recently, travel guide *Lonely Planet* listed it among the world's 'Top 10 Best Marine Encounters'. Graeme still enjoys hosting the tourists and skippering boats. 'I don't think he ever dreamed that 30 years later we'd all still be doing it,' says Vanessa.

1987 — the landmark year for what would become the swimming with seals experience — was also a landmark for Kaikōura's best-known attraction, whale watching. A group of local Māori from the local hapū of Ngāti Kuri, hit hard by the privatisation of the railways taking away jobs, mortgaged their homes to launch the venture despite some people labelling their plan crazy.

'No one is going to come to Kaikōura to watch whales. That was the feedback,' Whale Watch Kaikōura's general manager Kauahi Ngapora tells Katy Gosset. However, that first year 3000 did, and that became 100,000 a year pre-quake. 'Luckily they didn't listen to everyone saying it wouldn't work.'

No one knows what's going to happen now.

———

Kevin Keehan's mercy dash

'… the quake has pared things down to a bare
imperative — to be close to those you love.'
— Phil Pennington, RNZ *Insight*

Monday, 2.15pm

At Mt Lyford Lodge, fireman Hugh Wells gives me the hurry-up. 'We've just organised a ride with your pilot. You're picking up a guy to take back to Kaikōura to his family, who [he] hasn't had contact [with] since two o'clock or three o'clock this morning; and he's come a long way, he's come from Hawea to get to here.' The deadline of a 5pm live-cross into RNZ *Checkpoint* is also looming, and we're out of time. We don't get to see the wrecked stock inside, instead retracing our footsteps down the centre-line of the highway back to our chopper. It's a short hop this time, following the lead of Hugh's trail-biking partner, to Whalesback Station where, on the back lawn, two other choppers have already landed. I never do find out what they are there for. It occurs to Tim that having all this air traffic in an emergency zone, with many of the flights being pretty damn urgent to those on board or to those they're trying to reach, might not be ideal for safety. Later he asks a Defence Force guy about it, and is told it does look a little hairy. Later again, a pilot who's just flown in asks me if he was right in thinking he'd spotted civilian choppers taking off from the rugby ground, alongside the air force's NH90s. I say, that's right, they've been sharing that space, even though the top of the hill we're on has a lot of space. This pilot's not impressed. The civilian and military should be totally separate, he says; there is just too much potential for error with so many helicopters around.

However, another pilot — this time of a small plane who's on his 79th flight into Kaikōura two and a half weeks after the quake — tells me that he's been heartily impressed with virtually everyone's professionalism in concisely describing their position to others in the air in and around Kaikōura. Air force wing commander Scott McKenzie is equally generous: 'Everyone's been really great, talking on the radio, telling each other where they are. We just have to keep our eyes peeled, but it's great to see everyone pitching in, all hands to the pump, civilian operators, military operators working together.'

So, three choppers, blades whirring, in the backyard of the Whalesback farmhouse where we've come to pick up our evacuee. Looking at the modest, modern family home, it's clear that they would have been wishing they had built in wood and corrugated steel. The large masonry bricks have tumbled away from the walls in numerous places, exposing the building wrap beneath. Sliding deck doors are open, allowing a glimpse into a chaotic, dark living room and kitchen, where everything that could move and fall appears to have done just that. Countless living rooms, kitchens, pantries and bedrooms, both in Kaikōura and further afield, look just like this. Even if there had been time to pick through it all, and pick it all up, it's just not a priority. That's also clear from watching the small family group waiting in the chopper wash at edge of the lawn; they're standing close together, arms around one another. One is a big man in a Swanndri holding a small baby.

We don't get out; instead, one of the group, an old guy in a red-and-black Swannie, crabs across the lawn and climbs in. Kevin Keehan is our evacuee — not a medical but a mercy one. He's been driving for hours, hammering relentlessly up the island in the dark until dead-ending just 30 or so kilometres from Kaikōura. He can go no further. Yet he needs to make it through, which is where we come in.

Kevin lives in Kaikōura but works in Makarora at the head of Lake Wanaka. 'My wife rung me at two o'clock in the morning, and my daughter, and they said it was totalled. So I rung the boss. He picked me up in a tractor and brought me across the river.' This was so that he could get to where his short-wheel-base Land Cruiser with its dog trailer on the back was parked in the dark on the other side; they put his dogs in the front bucket of the tractor. 'I jumped in my truck, and I have just kept coming till I couldn't get any further. I drove up the riverbed, you see, 'cos I couldn't get further up the road, so I went up the riverbed. You have got to go fast or you sink.' Kevin laughs.

'Oh, I got through the riverbed, but the next slip stopped me completely, right there, up above Hugh's.' He points. 'And then there's more, and Hugh's just said to me he will jack up a ride and he's looking after my dogs, and that's what country people do: they look after everybody else.' Hugh and Jane Northcote farm almost 4000 hectares of some knee-achingly steep tussock hill country beside Mt Lyford. 'Oh, he's a top guy, but look at the state of everything around him.' Kevin indicates the fallen masonry. 'Yet he still gives the shirt off his back.' He tells me the big man clutching the wee baby is a farm employee. 'But I mean, Hugh just takes them into his circle, you know, everybody gets looked after.

'It's 8 hours' hard driving on a good day [from Makarora] and it's taken me 12 hours to get to Whalesback. I came round River Road because I knew I couldn't get across the Waiau Bridge, and then we get through Galletly's farm and then back onto the

Inland Road, and then I cut back up the Mason River and got to Whalesback … Oh yeah, I'm buggered, but I've still got to go deal with my family.' Kevin isn't sure what he's going to strike when he gets to town. He hasn't been able to talk to his father, who is 94 and deaf and blind. 'Somebody will be looking after him … They're my family, it's all I've got.'

That man deserves a beer, well done

— Charli Harrington, tweet

Goodonya Kev!

— Bruce McKay, tweet

With Kevin in the back, we head as the crow flies for Kaikōura airport, passing over pine plantations where trees have been knocked down. On the ground, we unload and squeeze into the double-cab of the ute we borrowed just this morning from Bob Dronfield. His precious boxes of health and safety planning material are still in it, thank God, but it means there's not a lot of room. Kevin sits on the tray to keep Bex's expensive video gear from bouncing off. We have 2 hours until we need to tell our story to *Checkpoint*, and we've got all these interviews and video to deliver to Wellington and no idea whether the damaged communications system will carry it. I drop Kevin home on the far side of town, just off Beach Road which doubles as State Highway 1. The road dead-ends at a small bridge that's fallen completely into the stream. Kevin points up the road to a pine shelterbelt, his place, and says, 'I'll walk from here.'

We get to see him again later when he tracks us down especially to offer us a hand — 'Whatever you need, whatever you need,' Kevin says. Running water and an internet connection at our hastily rented accommodation are off the menu, but he heads off to try to rustle them up for us anyway. Before he goes, he finishes his story for us: 'When I got home, everybody's standing; the old man's place was sweet as, he's happy as. Our place was pretty knocked around, in-laws' place was knocked around. They'd flown out to Christchurch and everybody's alive.'

At his dad's, there's not even any broken china. 'It's still standing, mate; standing in the middle of Rome, he reckons. It was like Hiroshima after the bombs: one chimney. Yeah, nah, it's just phenomenal to what it could have been. Yep, I think everybody was pleased to see everybody really. Even the cat was pleased to see me.'

——

Writing this, it's evident that there are gaps in these narratives. It's tempting to want to fill in all the holes in all the stories, to ring people up after the event and ask the questions I forgot on the day, or didn't ask to keep from interrupting someone in full flow. Such as, 'What's your boss's name, Kevin? And what do you do for a crust? And how old did you say you were?' But that would pretend to a completeness that wasn't there at the time, as if we and those we talked to were carefully dotting the i's and crossing the t's as we went along. Quite the opposite: just about everything on that Monday, Tuesday and Wednesday, especially, was seat-of-the-pants stuff, not just for us with our scrambled chopper flight, but also for the hundreds of families and individuals needing to improvise out of the blue to get hold of water, food, shelter and comfort — above all, comfort — and for the emergency services people faced with hundreds of tourists who within a crunching 120 seconds had gone from being the prime source of cash pumped into local tills to being an insupportable drain on the town's resources. So if there's a number-eight-wire feeling about these stories, that'd be right. It *is* number eight — stretched thin and tight across many strands, but working for us when it counts.

———

Down and out

'… it's obviously built up at a pretty rapid rate and that wall of water is moving down the river now'
— Richard McNamara, to RNZ, Nov 14

Monday, 3pm

We've got Kevin's story in the can, and Jenny's, and Claudene's, but if we aren't able to send the audio and video out for broadcast, it will count for very little. No one else will hear what they've been through. I drive through town to the South Bay turn-off, where Tim and Bex have been trying — and failing — to get a connection at a rest area picnic table out the front of the racecourse. We are in an information black hole in more ways than one: for instance, we don't know anything about the drama unfolding on the Clarence River a short hop north. At 4.40pm, RNZ carries this report:

> 'The Marlborough District Council says the slip dam on the Clarence River has breached and a large wall of water is heading downstream. Residents are urgently advised to move to higher ground immediately.'
> — RNZ, Facebook

The banked-up water on the Clarence bursts through the wall of debris. A helicopter spots the breach and calls it in. Initial reports are alarming — a wall of water up to 15 metres high is hurtling downstream — and it's said that people are being evacuated. Six kayaks and helmets are spotted on the riverbank downstream. A search for the kayakers begins. It's known that rafters, too, are on the river, though not precisely where. Richard McNamara of Marlborough Civil Defence tells John Campbell on RNZ *Checkpoint*: 'These [dams] generally do break within the first 24 hours, given the nature of them and the weight of water behind it. It looked like it was trickling out one side but it's obviously built up at a pretty rapid rate and that wall of water is moving down the river now.' John Campbell finishes the interview by warning: 'Get the hell away from the river.'

Genevieve King is one of the rafters. She's leading a group who have camped at Quail Flat halfway into a five-day trip that began at Hanmer. They are well upstream from the slip dam. She has no idea that they are the focus of an alert. 'We didn't really hear the news, but we were located quite quickly,' she tells me later. 'We had a satellite phone and we were near a homestead where they had a helicopter.' They are flown out, with Genevieve landing at her parents' badly damaged farm near the river mouth. The kayakers, meantime, are found safe and well, having left their gear and scrambled away from the river. The evacuation warning itself is rapidly downgraded.

'UPDATE: A group of kayakers thought missing on the Clarence River are safe'
— RNZ, tweet, Nov 14, 7.12pm

The first I hear about the rafters and kayakers is on the RNZ news bulletin at 5pm. With time again ticking by and no connection, we've reloaded the ute and scooted 400 metres along to another picnic table by the shell-and-gravel beach. The cloud is lowering, but the forecast gales have not eventuated. Rather, the sky is pearlescent, shimmering off the sea, and it feels like it might rain. Bex gets the video feed working and I'm patched into the studio on the cellphone, waiting to go live, and listening down the line to the news as it's broadcast. Just as I go to air, the video feed fails and the pictures from the beach are lost, but I press on as we still have the voice link:

'Well, good evening, John. Yeah it's been a long day, but not as long as for some. And as you can see we are actually on the shore of Kaikōura. We have just had an aftershock here. It's a beautiful scene, but it certainly made us flinch with that aftershock. It's not the worst we've felt today, though … A lot of houses are showing no signs of damage, although we have talked to local people who say that inside it's a different story. Many of the timber and iron houses, they have stood up fairly well. We did fly earlier over Elms Homestead … From the air, the iron is simply lying flat and the masonry and the bricks are flat … The centre of town is looking fairly normal except … there's hundreds and hundreds of people in the hospital park up by the medical centre, John; a lot of people dazed, a lot of people bewildered.'

— Phil Pennington, to John Campbell on RNZ *Checkpoint*, 5.15pm

———

Further afield

'We got smashed last time, and my husband and I made the decision: we're moving home to Te Anau next week. We've had enough'

— Robyn Dawson, of Awatere, to RNZ

Monday, outside Kaikōura

While we have been in Kaikōura, RNZ's Alex Perrottet has jumped on another chopper and flown into Marlborough. The grassy coastal headlands give little away, he reports:

A small slip here and there, nothing obvious to the untrained eye from the sky. Then GNS scientist Pilar Villamor, who has been marking her geological map, complete with fault-lines, sits up straighter and asks the pilot to slow down and descend.

The fault-lines are already drawn on the earth. A house is, so clearly, not where it is supposed to be. Villamor is excited, but contains it — realising the impact on the people we are about to meet. Sue and Richard Murray smile when we alight at Bluff Station, built on the Kēkerengū Fault. They warn us not to step on the power-lines strewn across the paddock.

Scott Waterman, a tall, wiry Englishman, got home at midnight 2 minutes before the ground beneath his house was ripped away. He was staying alone in a small white dwelling across the paddock from the homestead. It is now 2 metres higher and 10 metres away from where it used to be. Or perhaps the house is where it was and everything else around it has moved.

Sue and Richard walk me through the house, laughing at the busted grandfather clock lying face-down in the hall. In the lounge, they point out the broken china and glass — the carpet smelling of spoiled fine wine. They laugh. Every piece of furniture is upturned, paintings are smashed, and there are busted food packages all over the store room. A few chuckles more. 'You've just got to laugh,' Sue says. 'The petrol tank's fallen over, and we could smell that as soon as we came into the yard. There's no power, there's no phone, nothing. But we're all alive, and you start to realise how important it is.'

Next, Alex's chopper flies to Cheviot, where the overgrown rugby ground is in use as a helicopter refuelling station.

The only people around are a family offering coffee and tea to travellers. The woman's parents in Waiau have lost their house. The phones are down. Closed roads and a key bridge have cut off the town. There was nothing they could do, so they grabbed supplies and went to the rugby club. 'We just couldn't do anything at home, we were helpless and couldn't get through to Mum and Dad, so we just came down here to at least be useful,' the woman says. No one is able to help another mother who drives down to ask about water. Their mains are cut off, her children need to drink and she needs to clean.

NZ is such a village at times like this.

— Jolisa Gracewood, tweet, Nov 14

At Ward, Ross Ward is waiting for his luck to change. He tells RNZ's Tracy Neal that he and his wife, Helen Sangster, will never return to the wooden cottage they were living in, growing grapes on a 13-hectare Marlborough block. For now, they're living in a borrowed horse truck. 'We've been here 12 years, and we've had two floods, two earthquakes, a windstorm — we've both had issues with cancer. I'm a volunteer fire brigade member and they had some support people come in. As I said to them, "Why does my number keep coming up?"' says Ross.

At least nine families in the Marlborough district are forced out of their homes by the quake, the worst-hit of those around Ward and Seddon. Ross and Helen's cottage has been yellow-stickered. 'We'll go in for short periods of time, but as far as I'm concerned we'll never live in the house again. Not after that.'

Down the road, young farmers Tom and Angela Loe and their three children, aged five and under, are tenting while their nerves settle. It won't be the same for them at the historic family farm and homestay near Cape Campbell. 'Our farming practices are going to be tested or, if not, they'll have to change,' says Tom. 'We have done a lot of trading of stock, being so close to the main highway, so we'll have to re-strategise how we manage our farming practice.' Down the road at Yealands Estate vineyard, the cellar doors are shut for a few days, but no more than that.

'It was built to withstand an 8 on the Richter scale, so the building performed exactly as it should,' says chief operations officer Michael Wentworth.

Vicar Dawn Daunauda, in Seddon, is saying grace at a party for the Awatere Garden Club when Tracy visits. She is only just getting over the 2013 quake. 'For some, it is too much. They can't put the bricks back on again and keep on going. For me — I'm okay, but part of me is in denial.' Robyn Dawson, though, has had enough and is leaving Marlborough. 'We got smashed last time and my husband and I made the decision: we're moving home to Te Anau next week. We've had enough.' In the window of a local shop is a poster with a photo of a chihuahua: 'Missing since Monday 14th earthquake,' it says. 'Please contact if any sightings as she is very timid.'

———

The Māori wardens

'I have had no sleep all night, but I just want to get here and do this job, just help people.'
— Ari Boyd, to RNZ

Monday, 6.30pm

Leaving South Bay just after another live-cross at 6pm — John Campbell asks about the economic impact on the town, but we haven't even made it to the main street yet — we negotiate the slalom on the hill road caused by slumping of the tarseal, up to Churchill Park. We nickname it 'hospital park'. Hundreds of people are there. Cars and camper vans, many parked on the grass in front of the near-new hospital, surround it on three sides — to the north is Bad Jelly Backpackers and houses. No one will be fined for parking on the grass today. It is like a circling of the wagons, except that this threat cannot be kept at bay. Perhaps it's better understood as a holding of hands: research such as that being done at Canterbury University's psychology department suggests that feelings of powerlessness loom large after quakes, so staying close and holding tight provide comfort.

Ari Boyd's experience is a telling one. A Māori warden, she is standing in her high-viz yellow sleeveless vest under the entrance way to the hospital, overlooking the park sloping gently away. 'It was terrible, absolutely terrible,' Ari tells me. 'I just screamed, and then my husband went to the toilet and I thought he had collapsed, and I screamed out to my son to come and help pick him up, and then I, like, froze and my boy's, like, "You've got to get out, Mum." I couldn't move. And then I heard a car come up and I just ran. Just absolutely petrified.

'Went home this morning,' Ari continues. 'You know, it's a mess, but, hey, you can replace a TV, replace things — lives you can't — so I just closed the door, walked out. You know, it doesn't matter. I have had no sleep all night, but I just want to get here and do this job, just help people.'

In front of us, a bright red helicopter has set down on the grass. To the left are a couple of small tents and small satellite dishes — a TV crew is trying to send their material out. Later, one of them tells me that they succeeded in getting pictures on that night's 6pm TV news by the skin of their teeth. All around are cars and vans in which people have spent a sleepless night, and where many will sleep again for the next two nights to come. At the park's north end, there's a slice of normality where families are pushing children on swings; they give an occasional squeal of fun.

'… it's the first birthday I've ever missed'
— Keri King, to RNZ, Nov 29

The next day some of the town's children will be gone, evacuated from the disaster zone by air or road. At one school, St Joseph's, more than 20 of the 98 pupils leave. Bex snaps a photo of two girls and a boy sitting up on a ute cab's roof while waiting at a convoy checkpoint. Some of the parents who make this choice for safety's sake end up regretting it. Much later, Keri King tells RNZ's Kate Newton that when she put her three daughters, aged 9, 11 and 12, on the chopper that next morning, she assumed it would only be 'a week max'. Instead, she ended up missing the 11-year-old's birthday. 'I ummed and aahed about sending my children away. It got to the point where I was convinced.' The nine-year-old in particular was terrified by the shake and aftershocks, so the three went to stay with their aunt in Christchurch. Keri, also a Māori warden, stayed in Kaikōura to help. Hold-ups with fixing the Inland Road prevented convoys from getting people out or her children back to her. She tells Kate, 'I've got a nine-year-old daughter ringing me every second hour asking if the roads are open or if we've booked them on a flight. I had a daughter who turned 11 yesterday — it's the first birthday I've ever missed.'

Fang Yang sends her son, Mason, aged nine, to stay with his grandmother in Auckland. She tells Kate that this is so she can work long shifts at the health centre. 'I'm a nurse, that's my job, I can't go — there's no other option.' But Auckland's not a great option either. 'His grandma is 87 and can't manage … There's no one to help, so I have to get him back.'

Outside the hospital in the sun this Monday evening, Ari Boyd's friend Nancy sits in an orange plastic chair in her high-viz jacket. Two dozen or so people stretch in a line either side of her on a mini traffic island in the hospital car park, all with their eyes glued to their phones, tapping screens or trying to make calls.

'It just started shaking,' Nancy recalls of a few hours before, 'and I laid there in my bed and thought, "Oh, it will stop soon," but it didn't; it just got worse and worse. When I got up everything was just smashed, and I heard everything falling in the house. So I got in the truck and drove to my son's for my grand-daughter, and then we ended up on top of the hill.' Her voice breaks. I ask if she's been back home. 'Yep. My house is a mess, it's screwed, but we are all all right.' Nancy looks around at the people sitting in small groups in the park. 'They're all right,' she frowns, 'but some people need to learn to listen and be helpful. There's a marae set up, but they can only take so many. They're just going to have to sleep in cars 'cos they can't leave Kaikōura — the road's blocked every which way, so that's it.'

———

The Aussies and the charter

'So we decided, let's stick together, we're just going to stay in tents, stay in cars, and honestly, it's just a big camping trip for us right now, a big bonding experience.'
— Stephanie Wang, to RNZ

'I turn from a tourist into a refugee.'
— Bram Maas, to RNZ, Nov 15

Our attempts this Monday evening to send audio and visual material to RNZ in Wellington from outside the hospital fail. The district health board's free wi-fi is inundated. Piling into the ute, Bex and I head back to South Bay, repeating the slump-slalom but downhill this time, and carry on just past the turn-off, parking on the right in a large gravel lot outside Cave Tours and Café, not far from the airport. It's empty; inside, broken glassware and menus are scattered on the floor. We perch our laptops on the car bonnet and find a sweet spot. Just to keep us on our toes, however, a belter of an aftershock hits. It doesn't feel quite as large as the one at Mt Lyford Lodge, but it's enough to sound a warning crack and send ripples running the length of the polycarbonate sheeting above the café's deck. I'm just glad the roofing's made of plastic, not glass. A check on GeoNet shows two aftershocks at around 7.45pm, one a severe but shallow 5.6, and the other a 5.7, rated stronger as it's deeper. There will be more than 8000 aftershocks over the next 3 weeks.

It is an aftershock very like this that sends Stephanie Wang scampering out of The Albatross hostel for a second time, having already fled to the nearby hospital park after the 7.8 itself. 'We weren't sure if we wanted to stay in the hostel or stay in the tents ... 'cos we were expecting 140-kilometre [per hour] winds,' she tells Tim Graham. 'So we took down all the tents and went down to the hostel, and just as we were sitting at the hostel again there was an aftershock and we just sprinted right out of the hostel again. And we're, like, we're gonna go set up the tents, so we came back here, and I'd say we're pretty professional tent-setters.' Her group has seven small tents pegged up in the hospital park.

'Someone described it as it's like being at a music festival.' She laughs. 'Honestly, we're just with each other, we're having a good time, everyone's got such a great sense of humour. Some guys broke out the ukulele last night, we were having a jam session. It's fun, making the most out of what we've got.' The hostel staff got them safely to the park where people were handing out blankets. They hung out at picnic tables. 'We were waiting for an assessment on our hostel to see if it's safe to go back in ... but we just feel way safer out here, plus we're all with each other, we have each other right here.'

A little earlier, outside a portable toilet at the park, Bex met the Barker family and Billy the Goat. The family rescued the four-month-old kid when its mother was shot. Billy goes everywhere with them — including up the hill early on Monday, where the five of them, plus Billy, huddle in their car. Unnerved by the quake, Billy won't let them out of his sight.

'He's still very attached to us, especially my daughter Annalise — the night of the quake he would only stop making noise when she got back in the car,' says Karana Barker. Later, the family, their house destroyed, camp out at friends', and Billy finds love in a nearby paddock with a goat named Lucky. Lucky fell down a cliff during the quake and had to be rescued by her owner a few days later.

> 'Now, he follows them everywhere.'
>
> — the story of Billy the Goat, RNZ

Down the hill outside the Cave Tours café, an SUV pulls up on the grass bordering the beach on the far side of the highway. Stewart Menzies of Melbourne unloads his five-month-old son, Fletcher, and a buggy. His wife, Hayley, is on the phone, arranging a fixed-wing charter flight for the next morning at nine. It'll cost $2000 for seven of them, but they say it's worth it.

'It is what it is,' says Hayley. 'We have quickly run out of supplies, there's no food options in town, just about out of nappies for Fletcher, so we have come to Kaikōura airport to try and see if we can get on a charter flight back to Christchurch — or just about anywhere really, just to get out. We saw the images of the road on the news tonight and decided that there wasn't going to be any way out in the next 24 hours, so we would take action into our own hands.'

She's right: it's Friday before a convoy of 27 army trucks makes it into town over the busted Inland Road. A couple of days before, a civilian truck becomes the very first to make it through, with 16,000 litres of water for the hospital. A loader shoves rocks out of its way, a digger helps it ford riverbeds rather than go over dodgy bridges, and two geotech engineers keep watch on landslides as it drives around or across them.

'QUAKE LATEST: Army aid convoy with essential supplies finally arrives in Kaikoura'
— RNZ, headline, Nov 18, 5.24pm

Load up that Humvee with pies and beers
— Nigel Mahoney, tweet

Hayley adds that some Chinese tourists staying at the same motel as them haven't had to look out for themselves. 'The Chinese embassy … have paid for all the Chinese groups who were here to be flown out by helicopter.' She laughs, and says she must get on the phone to Malcolm Turnbull. It turns out that this evacuation has been going on for most of the day from on top of a hill above town. It's the first I've heard of the Chinese operation. It points to what will become the dominating story of Kaikōura day 2: the airlift. I leave the Menzies, pushing Fletcher in the buggy, the sun going down behind the scarred hills behind South Bay, on a day they'll never forget and wish they'd never experienced.

———

Fish and chips, but no beer

'If you do want to come out and see me that would be fine, even if it's only to try one of our beers.'
— Max Scattergood invites an RNZ news crew over

Monday, 8:45pm

Up at the hospital park, car and van windows are misting up as people begin their second night of quake vigil. As night falls, swathes of the town remain dark because the power is still cut off. Fortunately, we have our hastily rented house in Mount Fyffe Avenue, with power and (albeit intermittent) water. It doesn't, however, have any towels and not a scrap of food. A bath mat can be used to get dry after a shower, though — crikey, a shower! We should be thankful. And we are: thankful, but hungry. The chippies and nuts we've snacked on have been it so far today, so we head back out to find a meal.

A full 21 hours and several nerve-wearing aftershocks after the 7.8, we are driving around town trying to find a feed. Food is primarily what's on our mind, but as we pass one dark takeaway, restaurant or pub after another it occurs to me that we'd also be out of luck if we were wanting a drink. There is no beer to be had. Say that again: a provincial New Zealand town in the stunned aftermath of its violent birth into a new normal, and there is no beer to be had. Unless you have a fridge at home — but then, with the power off, the beer would be getting warm. I'd have expected a pub or two to have flung wide their doors and to be doing a roaring trade in settling the nerves. But families want to stick close at times like this. Parents want to be by their children, children by their elderly parents, lovers by each other's side. And the police don't want to be out on the street dealing with someone who's put away a few too many just trying to take this unprecedented edge off. No one needs 'drunk and disoriented' right now, so it's probably a good thing that neither we, nor anyone else, can find a beer to buy.

Max Scattergood, who runs Kaikōura Brewing Company, sheds light on the situation during my second trip to the town.

'Only when [the beer] is back chilled will I know if I can salvage any of that and maybe get some sold. But I only have a couple of hundred bottles in stock, so will have to try to recycle those, as it may be quite some time before I can get a pallet from Blenheim. So sorry, but if you do want to come out and see me that would be fine, even if it's only to try one of our beers.'

Another person struggling to cope is the storekeeper at the dairy on the main street, West End. It is the only shop we find open in the whole of the town on that first Monday. We had swung by a bit earlier while it was still light. The dairy is gloomy inside and there are towels over the ice cream in the freezer. People come and go. I popped in hoping to interview the storekeeper — but she's stressed and can't manage it, though she tells me they have sold out of bread, and frozen bread, and milk, and water — and I forget to buy any food there.

Tim Golden, who runs the Sunrise Lodge to the north of the town, is walking by with two women backpackers from America. 'This is the first time I've come down to have a look,' he says. 'I've been looking after everybody I've got to look after, now I'm going for a walk. There's a dairy that's got its doors open but the lights are not on, there's not much else going on. We have got 21 international visitors, so we will be looking after them, pulling together our food … Anything that's in the freezer is going to go off, so we will just cook it on the barbecue 'cos we've got gas. We got some water from the service station — they were nice enough to sell us some if we could pay cash.'

Now, after 9 on Monday night, even the dairy is shut. West End is dark and deserted — almost. A light's on in a fish and chip shop, and a huddle of people are at a table. It's a TV news crew. We make to go in, but the woman at the counter gestures no, and one of the TV team gives us a death stare. Another of the team comes out and offers us a few chips in a bit of paper. The encounter is the one bum note on a day characterised by people's good humour and generosity in speaking to us, even when they're a little dazed

— and, in the case of Bob Dronfield, offering us his double-cab ute, too. Bob also lets the next RNZ crew that comes in to replace us late on Wednesday use his ute and, what's more, he brings in some fuel for them — though on the Thursday he grabs the truck so that he can take a crew up the Inland Road to fell trees that could be a risk to the convoys. Later I learn of a bum note for Bob, too: someone breaks into his yard and nicks his chainsaw fuel. The police get involved. There's always a chance that the thief will think it's regular fuel and put it in their car. That'd be justice.

—

The chef and the crayfish

'We're here to help, we'll help anybody. We're not here to give up.'
— Major Timms, to RNZ, Nov 14, 10pm

tino pai mahi!
— Emma Kitson, tweet

Monday, 9.30pm

If we're going to eat, we have no choice but to head up to the marae, though I hadn't wanted to add to their already substantial burden. When we get to it, just behind the hospital, 30 or so tourists are already bedded down in sleeping bags and blankets on mattresses on the floor of the dining room. It's early, but they're exhausted; there's not a peep out of them. Others are sleeping in other rooms. Thank God the marae has electricity — whether it's mains supply or from generators I forget to ask. It doesn't bear thinking about what would've happened if it, or the hospital a stone's throw away, had had their supply cut off. The fluorescents burn brightly in the kitchen where the Takahanga Marae crew are slumped in chairs, facing a clean-up of the evening meal after what's already been a 21-hour day for them. Marae deputy chair and kaumātua Major Timms is so tired that his eyes have closed to slits and he can barely speak, but he does so anyway when I ask him how many he's fed. He sighs heavily. 'Oh, about 700 people this afternoon … The whole lot of us, not just me, a whole group of us, they've all done well … We have plenty of helpers here, they were awesome, awesome.' A tall, bearded guy comes in and offers to help up with the dishes and wipe-down. I ask Major Timms if he had heard Prime Minister John Key earlier guessing that the repair bill could hit at least \$2 billion. 'No, I didn't hear John at all today, I was too busy here.' And the task won't ease up anytime soon. Over the next several days, Major Timms's crew serves up 10,000 meals and gives out 1700 care packages.

'It's like you are a refugee,' says Bram Maas, of the Netherlands, who is sleeping in his car. 'I turn from a tourist into a refugee. But there is also for me the other side of the coin, you meet people in different ways … I feel cared for. This is life, things can change rapidly. This is an experience … I try to be as normal as possible, just accept the situation and pursue my holiday on a smaller scale.'

Our three-person team is among those the marae feeds this Monday night. Major's son Jason Timms is also at the large stainless-steel table in the kitchen. A chef, he winds up doing a lot of the heavy work of the cooking. Almost as an afterthought, Jason offers us the nugget of the day: Local crayfishers have 1.5 tonnes — tonnes! — of cray in their holding tanks that they now can't either get to market or sell locally, as all the restaurants are closed. They've begun donating it. 'Come and look at this,' Jason tells us, and opens up the cool-store door.

'I've got about three or four hundred crays in here,' says Jason. 'Normally it'd be getting dispersed to all the restaurants in town. 'Cos I'm a chef at the Adelphi Restaurant, and I just cooked up 100 kilos … and now I've got to do some more … Actually, I had all my staff up here today, helping out. I called up all the chefs around town and they all come up and help me out.' So, crayfish for breakfast, lunch and dinner? Jason chuckles: 'From breakfast on, all day, all day.' I suggest some people might come back for thirds. 'So they should, after I've finished with them!' Later, the Timms, father and son, are jointly nominated for New Zealander of the Year, The People's Choice by the *New Zealand Herald*.

> Awww tu meke guys! I have happy memories of
> staying at this marae, especially eating the best hangi
> ever (well except for Grandad's of course)
> — Pip McDonald, tweet

After editing our material at the rented house, it's approaching midnight. This is the first 24-hour day I have worked, and Tim and Bex look similarly shattered; but the end is in sight. The Earth, however, is not done with us quite yet. An aftershock hits like a whiplash. It doesn't roll, it just cracks. Our chairs go flying as we race for cover. I crouch in a doorway. We brace for more, but there isn't any. The shake is over very suddenly, not so the feeling of uncertainty and powerlessness, which intensifies; it portends a broken night's sleep ahead, just as if everyone was living with an enormous, teething 12-month-old in the next bedroom.

And we still have our audio and pictures to get through to Wellington. For us, this has become a sequence of jumping between the stepping stones of unseen and only guessed-at portals that might provide enough signal to connect with producers and programme and bulletin editors in Wellington and Auckland. Earlier, we had got lucky at the car park outside the Cave Tours café, and on the beach at South Bay. Now, we try again outside the hospital: with most of the tourists asleep in their cars and vans, the load is off the DHB's wi-fi, so we rapidly complete our last job of the day.

3

TUESDAY:
GETTING OUT AND GETTING ON

'It's a sight to behold … this is David Attenborough
stuff.'

— Winston Gray, to RNZ, Nov 15, 7.45am

'I hug them when I leave.'

— Xaolai Che, to RNZ, Nov 15

The mayor and the honeymooners

'I think people are feeling fairly dirty … there hasn't
been a lot of showering going on … Our neighbour
has filled up his pots and pans, he offered us a bath;
he heated it up on his barbecue last night.'

— Phil Pennington, to RNZ

Tuesday, 6.30am

After a broken night's sleep, we rise early and drive back to the
hospital park. A wake-up call is sounded by a red-and-white
helicopter landing on the grass. The pilot tells me he's with the
Marlborough Lines company and is heading back to Blenheim to
help get the power back on. Groggy tourists emerge from misted-
up cars, stretching to get the kinks out of their backs. The RNZ
studio calls up for a live-cross into *Morning Report*:

'I'm outside the hospital and what I can see is
we have got more than 100 vehicles outside the
hospital, just like there's been from last night; at
least 20 of them are camper vans, there's a Kiwi
Experience bus … People are just waking up … it
has been a very uneasy night, I know. An aftershock
last night about midnight of 5.1 sent us running for
the doorways, and there's been a large one this
morning. Rained very heavily overnight, but as
I say the weather will be key — we expect 40 or

50 choppers to be coming in, primarily using the
rugby ground that's down below the hospital …

What we have got is 1200 people on top of the usual
loading of 2000 — and that might be like Wellington
looking after 70,000 people, Auckland looking after
half a million — looking for food, looking for water and
there's not enough to go around … So that means the
tourists, they want to get out; they are desperate to
escape the aftershocks … [The town's] been looking
after them, but it does need them to go to lessen the
load, and they want to go.'
— Phil Pennington, to RNZ, Nov 15, 7.20am

On no one is lost the irony of a tourist town that needs the
tourists to leave. And that's just what they have been doing,
though we had been missing it. The Menzies the night before
had mentioned the exodus of Chinese tourists being under way
already. Now, when I glance up at a hill above the town after
talking to the radio, I spot them: a large group of people outlined
against the sky. As I watch, a small helicopter — it looks like
a Robinson bubble-type — swoops in and sets down. We need
to get up there now, I tell Tim and Bex. It's all of 2 minutes in
the ute up Shearwater Drive, past a sign announcing Seaview
Kaikōura — a suburb of new, flash, solid-looking homes —
then a left into Miromiro Drive, and there, behind the partially
poured concrete foundations of another new home, we see the
impromptu helipad in the grass.

'And a chopper's just coming in now on these suburban heights — South Pacific Helicopters — this is in a new subdivision above Kaikōura ... I guess it'll be taking people off ...'

— Phil Pennington, to mic, Nov 15, 7.45am

Dan is with the ground crew of Tekapo Helicopters, just one of three or four chopper companies using the hill. 'We've got our two aircraft here today: we've got a four- and a six-seater doing constant trips throughout the day, as long as this weather continues to hold,' says Dan. 'This group here numbers between 50 and 60 at the moment, but there are a lot of other people stuck here ... who may need help during the day.'

Kaikōura mayor Winston Gray is already here. Thirty-six hours and a snatch of sleep on, he looks chipper in a check shirt; certainly more presentable than we are. The sun glinting off his balding head reminds me that I don't have a hat, or any sunscreen. The mayor is watching as four Chinese nationals get aboard the Robinson. During the course of Monday, helicopters chartered by the Chinese government have already lifted perhaps 60 people off from here, and they will shift scores more on Tuesday until the exodus is virtually complete by that evening. It's hugely impressive, particularly the speed with which the Chinese consulate is able to let its nationals know about the flights out — all paid for, too.

The mayor says that locals aren't short of back-up, either. 'Support's been great. Yesterday Gerry Brownlee, John Key and Andrew Little [were] in, so they've actioned the [military] helicopter thing, and the [Navy frigate] *Canterbury*, so we really appreciate that. The Hurunui, of course they've got their issues, but they're working with us. I got a call, you know, from the top of the North Island down — if you need anybody, we'll get it to you. So we're probably quite well-off. The key thing is the engineering side, to check those bridges out through to Waiau, the buildings through time, the commercial stuff, some residential.'

The scope of the support extends to a bunch of artists who band together to put out some postcards with a seaside Kaikōura theme. One shows an octopus in a diver's helmet that reminds me of a hard hat. Designer Stephen McCarthy did a similar thing to raise money for Christchurch's recovery, creating posters of historic buildings that were demolished there. He feels connected to the latest upheavals. 'Kaikōura is our place to escape — surfing at Meatworks, spearfishing down from the tunnels, surfcasting on the shingle beach at Peketa campground.' Hostel owner Dave Stanford speaks for a lot of locals when he says thanks for the support: 'It's been overwhelming, from the government down … it couldn't be more of a wrap-around package.'

> It feels like a puppy would help a lot of people.
> #EmergencyCute
> — RNZ tweet

Winston Gray tells me he returned to the town on Monday afternoon, driving as far south along State Highway 1 as he could before a chopper picked his party up. 'We got to Clarence at three o'clock yesterday, and that was a challenge getting down from Blenheim, you know. Some of the road's dropped a foot off the bridges, then we struck a piece where the road has lifted 20, 30 feet, and that stopped us … It runs out to sea, a new reef has formed … There are pāua there on a rock-face that's a metre and a half out of the water … It's a sight to behold … this is David Attenborough stuff. I think I made a comment on Facebook "Mother Earth scratched her back".

'That's my old farm up there on the left.' He points northwest towards the Seaward Kaikōura Range. 'That's all new … There's an iconic hut in the valley through there, Barratt's Hut, that many a tramper that climbs Manakau [uses]. My son flies: he says you want to have a look in there, the whole landscape's changed in there.'

The mayor tells me the latest he knows about the road and water, and it's clear he's taking an optimistic line, intimating that things will be back up and running soon. I take this chat as my Civil Defence briefing for the next few hours. Reporting from the ground like this, our priority is to record the face-to-face interviews that can't be done remotely. Emergency briefings, on the other hand, are always accompanied by press releases and communications people who can be raised by phone from our office in Wellington or Christchurch, so we leave that up to them. It turns out that the office has a lot on their plate, though: Wellington has just started flooding.

Tim Graham is talking to Chinese tourists who are abuzz at the prospect of getting out. Che Xaolai, from Fujian province, got married in October. 'We are going honeymoon now. This is third day we come to New Zealand, and earthquake come, and so we have to go on our travel. If we got to Christchurch we can go other place, too. I'm afraid this is amazing honeymoon,' Xaolai says with a laugh.

She adds: 'I'm a little frightened … [In Fujian] we always have earthquake, but is just a small … I just feel a little shake and it is gone. But in New Zealand I feel like, wow, it is big shaking and I is frightened, and I think house maybe fall down to the ground, so I just run away. But the house in New Zealand very strong … We were going to sleep at midnight … I feel like the house is shaking and I don't know what happened, and then a glass fell to the ground and [broke], and we just came out of the house … I get help from the people … They give me some food and water and coffee … I hug them when I leave.'

Xaolai says that all of the Chinese tourists in town head to the hospital, where someone from the Chinese consulate — somehow or other, it's not clear — tells them to go up the hill to be evacuated. 'Nobody tell me I have to pay the money, maybe not.'

It's approaching 8am, and another live-cross into *Morning Report* looms. But the cellphone signal on the hill is weak, so I drive back down to the hospital park. No signal here either, and the hospital declines to let me use their landline. It's 8.01am. When

I yell out in the car park to ask if anyone among the two dozen tourists on their screens has a phone line up, most ignore me and one or two look at me like I'm a crazy man. Running back to the ute, I'm redialling and redialling. 8.05am. My hand is on the door handle when my call goes through. Phew. I tell listeners I've just been up at the hill-top exodus.

'Winston Gray is up there — he's very happy that they're happy to be going. He's happy also that the supplies and stress on the town is easing, although he's happy to be able to look after them … The water supply is an issue. They have got a couple of tanks; they don't know what's happened below them — if there's been any subsidence. They don't know the quality of the water so they are suggesting people buy bottled water or boil it. They are saying they could open the old aquifers if they had to, up in the foothills. Power is an issue. Some of the town got power last night; where we are it was off again this morning.'

— Phil Pennington, live-cross to RNZ *Morning Report*, Nov 15, 8.16am

————

The unhappy evacuees

'I think they underestimated the capacity. They thought people [would] stay here and wait, wait until the roads are okay and then continue their holiday. That's not the reality.'

— Silve Casanellas, to RNZ, Nov 15

— Debbie Betteridge, to RNZ, Nov 15, 8.45am

Tuesday, 8.30am

I join Tim and Bex, and we walk a very short distance from the hospital park to the marae. It's a lovely setting: at the end of a short, leafy cul-de-sac behind a rustic fence, with tracks leading down through trees to the seaside streets below, and a glimpse too of the Pacific Ocean. At any other time, tourists would wander idly through here, some stopping by the marae curious to learn more about Māori culture, others on their way down to Dive Kaikōura, the esplanade motels or the beach itself on the north side of the peninsula. Not now, however; at this moment several hundred people are milling about in the road around a series of tables and a chair on which a Civil Defence man in an orange vest is standing, telling them how they need to register for a military chopper flight out. He cuts a lonely figure of officialdom; I've not seen more than perhaps two police officers standing at the verge, and at one stage glimpsed a chap in an army uniform, but just the one.

The Civil Defence chair-man doesn't have a megaphone and it's evident that not everyone can hear him. 'Here is the process,' he calls out. 'Is anyone here pregnant?' He carries on after a bit: 'Who are we going to take? Well, probably three of us are going to take your details, if you really need to get out today.

The priority will be given to medical conditions, young children, elderly, and then the rest. Is that fair?' There's a murmuring of assent and a few 'yeahs'.

'You will come up here,' the CD man continues, talking to the crowd that's all around him, 'two or three … We will ask for your name and home address. We will ask your priority. If we catch one straight away, that needs to go straight away, they will go straight to the gathering area there and be first on the next one down. Okay? That's the fairest way I can do it. If you're not priority I'll ask you to please wait, we do have your name and we'll see how we go.'

A woman who sounds French speaks up, asking about those with connecting flights. 'You're a priority as well,' the CD man says, 'but not over medical, okay?' A grey-haired British woman asks how old is elderly. He's not sure, or at least he's not clear. I can't help thinking that the qualification age will get lower the more someone complains. And some people *are* feeling agitated; there's that underlying feeling you get at an airport check-in counter where people are a little on edge that the queue is too long and the time is too short.

Ron Schwach of Germany had put his name down for evacuation on Monday night: 'There seems to be a second list now, and I'm not sure about it,' he says. 'Nobody seems to know — every person you talk to tells you a different thing,' says a young woman with a Geordie accent. An airport check-in is one thing, but an aftershock-hit holiday another. In the street outside the marae, most people are doing an admirable job of keeping their anxiety in check, though everyone's threshold for personal disaster management is different.

So when a tall, thin, greying man, a New Zealander, tells me to 'f— off — you shouldn't be talking to these people, these people are waiting to get out', I try not to bite back. I think he believes I'm causing people distress; it may be that he's well-meaning. A short, bearded guy leaning on a car hears him and comes to my aid, interjecting that early on Monday 'Radio New Zealand was the first one we were listening to in the car'. He introduces himself as Damer Farrell. He took photos for the *Greymouth Star* for three decades, and is here with a young local boy: 'This is Tahi … he has a really bad heart condition which requires lots of medication, but we'll sort it out.' The boy will be on an early flight out.

Not so Belgian tourist Silve Casanellas. He's unhappy, and you can't really blame him. Silve's on his honeymoon, too, just like Che Xaolai up on the hill, and the similarities end there. He tells me it's a compliment to the Chinese government what it's been able to achieve, and adds caustically, 'and a big compliment to the New Zealand government that they are not able to do what the Chinese are able in their own country.

'We have a hotel at the coastline,' says Silve. 'You feel every shake, every tremble, so what will you do? We slept two days in the mountain in the car. The first day we were six people in one car, last night we were four persons in a car … I think they underestimated the capacity. They thought people [would] stay here and wait, wait until the roads are okay and then continue their holiday. That's not the reality — 80 or 90 per cent of the people want to go straight away home after this experience, and I think they totally underestimated that.'

He has only praise for the marae and locals, but brickbats otherwise. 'We are 32 hours later. We make yesterday a list, the list vanishes. We make new list … Who are here by country, by people? They don't know nothing … it is chaos. Even at this moment I don't feel somebody's really in charge, really making a list of priorities. I don't feel there's organisation, and if it's in a Third World country I can expect that, but this is New Zealand — where's the military, where's the people in charge? I see a lot of choppers flying around … Politically, army-wise, it should be very well organised and it is not that at all.'

Nearby, surprisingly, is Hayley Menzies, with baby Fletcher and Stewart. They cancelled the expensive charter flight she had booked when they heard about the free military ones. Now they're in a small group at the top of a path down the hill to the rugby ground where the NH90s will take off from, so it looks like they'll be out soon. 'We found out late last night that we were able to register to be evacuated from here, so we came down and did that,' Hayley says. 'And they told us to be here at eight o'clock with all our luggage. So when we got here there were 600 other people here and they said that initially there was 400 people that put their names down and then another 300 this morning, so essentially there were 700 people who wanted to get out today … all with reasons why. So, we've been waiting and waiting. They said that they might open the Inland Road out of here but they won't let us know until 12 o'clock today.

'I think it's been quite ordinary myself, like I don't know why someone didn't sit with a laptop and electronically register everybody last night so then they had everyone's details … so then they just sort of sort it and prioritise from there. Because now we've had to list our names all again and everyone is lining up again and, you know, there's lots of foreigners who can't speak English, and people pushing … There's been some Red Cross and some police officers, but even then, like, a lot of the people at the back couldn't hear because they didn't have a proper, like a megaphone sort of thing, so everybody's quite confused and unsure about what's actually going on. I guess the only thing in our favour is that it's not raining.'

Leanne Foulds, from Auckland, tells Tim she just wants to leave. 'I think there was a little bit of higgledy-piggledy actually for a while. I don't know if they've got their planning quite right. But, in saying that, I understand they weren't prepared for anything this big.'

Debbie Betteridge is an Englishwoman who lives in France; she's taking a very pragmatic view: 'I think you just have to find your own means to get the information. The information is not flowing, if you know what I mean. So we've done that, mainly through contacts at home,' she laughs. ''Cos *we* know the ship arrives this evening, but that's through our Home Office and through my son in England phoning around and stuff ... And now suddenly we're told we can't take luggage [on the military chopper] which, had we known that, you know what I'm saying, we would've packed differently this morning or whatever, but it's very difficult.'

———

The warning that wasn't

'We've had several tsunami warnings when there was no tsunami ... That causes a lot of cynicism.'
— Bruce Rogan, Mangawhai, to RNZ

Complications, glitches and mistakes insert themselves into the quake response from the word go. A tweet from the national Civil Defence centre at 1.11am on Monday says, 'We are having issues with our website. We will be posting info on Twitter ...' With the Kaikōura evacuation, the early signs aren't good, but it ends up surprisingly rapid and error-free — by the Wednesday night, most of those who want to go are gone. On a hot hill-top this Tuesday morning, though, people like Silve, Debbie, Hayley and Leanne seem to have a point about whether Civil Defence, and ultimately the government, really have a good enough handle on the immediate emergency response. Especially given that the country gets more than its fair share of both practice and the real thing.

> 'All New Zealanders have to be aware of what the
> environment they're living in is. And this is it: we live in
> the shaky isles, we live on a plate boundary.'
> — Ken Gledhill, to RNZ, Nov 16

Following a 7.9 quake in 2009, Civil Defence was ordered to review its response to a Pacific Ocean tsunami alert because it was not good enough. It worked to improve matters. Even so, the response seems to be only part of the way to being good enough — at 12.30am on November 14, sirens sounded in the Far North while at Lyall Bay in Wellington, which opens directly onto Cook Strait, no sirens sounded and the international airport stayed open. In Mangawhai, Bruce Rogan rolled over and turned a deaf ear — cramming his good one into the pillow. 'We've had several tsunami warnings when there was no tsunami,' he told RNZ's Lois Williams. 'That causes a lot of cynicism. People say, well, this is just Dad's Army, trying to justify their existences.' RNZ reports GeoNet saying that sirens are not a great option anyway, and calling for extra funding to staff its monitoring centre 24 hours a day so that a person and not a machine decides what to do in the event of a quake.

> 'The person is actually woken up potentially out of
> a deep sleep to suddenly make really vital decisions.

At the moment the best practice internationally is that you have people awake making that decision, not the machines because the machines will make too many false detections.'

— GeoNet director Ken Gledhill, to RNZ, Nov 16, 12.04pm

It all gets a bit embarrassing on November 24, when West Coast Civil Defence issues an urgent warning about a possible 'large aftershock' striking the region, then retracts it, then has National Civil Defence distancing itself from the whole business.

If nothing else, this sets up a lot of quivering on social media. 'Feel it's time to keep off fb, [anxiety's through] the roof with all these other site predictions … reading stuff saying they think the alpine is getting ready to go off scares the crap outa me,' is one Facebook post that evening. Another: 'My son was very upset watching this … there are lots of frightened people out there and reporting stuff like this just makes my anxiety worse.' It's not as if New Zealand has a monopoly on patchy responses, though: Hurricane Katrina was not exactly an advertisement for the competence of America's plethora of emergency agencies back in the day.

On December 22, the government announces a $3 million increase in funding for GeoNet, saying that planning work for a 24/7 warning centre is already under way.

The All Blacks touch down

''Cos if there were someone hurt here, we were
buggered — because you couldn't go anywhere and
we had no communication, so we [would've] had it.'
— James Murray, to RNZ

'I'm scared and worried — it's my family's future.'
— Penny Betts, to RNZ

Doing the right thing, at the right time — every time — when so
much is going on, is too much to expect. The international media
gives Richie McCaw big marks for trying when the All Black
captain turned chopper pilot swings into action early on Monday,
ferrying fire service and USAR (Urban Search and Rescue) workers
here and there. This is not Christchurch, though, with multi-storey
buildings where people are or may be trapped, so the USAR people
have little to do. About the only pile of masonry in Kaikōura is
at the Elms Homestead, where the rescue work is already done.
This remarkable lack of visible damage to homes and buildings in
Kaikōura makes me think I'd rather be in my suburban home or a
single-storey town than a big city when a big one hits.

The Guardian in the UK likes the McCaw story: 'The former
All Blacks great Richie McCaw, who is now a commercial pilot
after retiring from rugby in 2015, has been flying rescue workers

in the wake of the quake,' it says at 5.30pm on the Monday. CNN is also a fan: 'The double World-Cup-winning captain witnessed the damage first-hand and noted the impact on the surrounding landscape. "The actual township's OK but the roads in both directions — there's slips and stuff all over the place," said McCaw.' Three of the 14 paragraphs of the story are about the All Blacks, not the quake.

One fixed-wing pilot carrying in supplies gratis for a church group in Kaikōura is told he'll be going to heaven. He tells me he's not sure he wants to be in heaven if the woman who talked the entire way in on the 40-minute flight from Christchurch to Kaikōura will be there. In a disaster zone there are lots of ways to be appreciated, and lots of ways to not be. It might have been thought that Richie was just popping in to say 'gidday' to the kids at Waiau School — which is how he described his assistance — when he could have done more.

Another ex-All Black, Sir John Kirwan, flies into Kaikōura in late November. He's a mental health ambassador and tells a crowd they're resilient. 'Keep looking after yourselves and find joy in the little things,' he says. 'A lot of people start to get worried about their anxiety and fear. It's about normalising it instead of trying to bottle it up — it's good to cry, good to hug, good to talk about it — especially with the kids.'

Penny Betts, who runs a store on the main street, tells RNZ's Sally Murphy that things have indeed been overwhelming. "Red

Cross have just been in here to help me clean up my shop. It's the first time I've been in it, because I couldn't face it. I'm just trying not to get angry and impatient to wait for the insurance things to kick in. I know it's going to take time. I'm scared and worried — it's my family's future.'

Being there — popping in to show you care — is half the battle, for the long haul and the short. In the immediate aftermath, at least the country's most famous pilot Richie McCaw *does* pop in, at Waiau School and elsewhere. By contrast, no one lands at James and Becky Murray's farm above the Clarence River after the shake; in fact, says James, no one from Civil Defence ever comes by, by air or by road. Their farm, situated on a high point, is a natural refuge and all 40 or so locals hike up there. 'The quake, she sort of hit and within about half an hour everybody ended up at our place,' James tells me. 'We all ended up here and lit a bonfire under the tree and all got some chairs and rocked her out, which was really good, it was awesome, 'cos that's a real country thing … The great thing about everybody arriving here, we knew who we had to go and look for … So we knew everybody was accounted for and that was really important.

'Next morning there was probably about 20 choppers and bloody planes going everywhere, and the thing that frustrated me [is] I don't think people knew how bad it was, and because everything was cut quickly, the telephone cables was cut that quick 'cos the rise in the land happened at 3 kays a second, it was unbelievable, and there was no communication … Yeah, all these choppers around and I think in hindsight … if Civil Defence had put a chopper out and gone to certain points they would've found out pretty quickly how people were and if there was anybody hurt. 'Cos if there were someone hurt here we were buggered, because you couldn't go anywhere and we had no communication, so we [would've] had it. And that's something that really needs looking at, in my book.'

The Clarence River Rafting company has satellite phones which could have helped, but James doesn't know this. I realise that our chartered chopper is one of the ones that has flown over them, around 11am on the Monday, and we didn't think to stop either.

Neighbours like Rick and Julia King have much the same story, though for them it was worse. Not only did the choppers not stop, but they also upset the deer which ran out through their busted perimeter fences. The couple don't know how many they've lost, taking off like this, or how many are dead. Their grown children, William and Genevieve, go online with a plea to pilots to avoid the Kings' river flats on the severely ruptured limestone of the Clarence's south bank, and by and large, after a while they do.

South of Kaikōura, Alastair Trewin at Glenstrae Farm 4 Wheeler Adventures goes through the same experience: a swarm of choppers in the air but not a single one landing at their spread, isolated on State Highway 1 by slips. Two houses end up red-stickered and a third is marginal. Alastair has limited cellphone reception in the dark after midnight, but that mightn't have helped his brother if he'd been stuck in his old farmhouse when all the chimneys collapsed. He's not stuck, though; they're all okay. 'But it was only luck,' says Alastair. He and James Murray want local input into any official debrief about the response. Civil Defence tells me, on December 9, that it's a little early to be talking about debriefing.

Up over the hills in the Hurunui, I hear of another farmhouse where five old chimneys fell down. Fortunately, the family lives in a renovated section of the sprawling house. Those chimneys that didn't fall in the quake might well come down after it, though; my neighbour in the Hutt Valley tells me in early December that he's had an $800 quote to have his taken down and the bricks removed. He'll probably go for it; I'm thinking about taking my own chimney down myself.

Patchy is the best way to describe the response, like a bike tyre with punctures in some spots and patches on top of each other in others. So many helicopters landed in fields inland up the Clarence River, beyond the failed bridge, that locals feel the responders were tripping over each other and wonder whether there was any coordination going on. At Kēkerengū, Pip Todhunter's farm remains cut off until late November, but she says things aren't too bad at all. 'We've had a huge amount of supplies being dropped off.'

Queuing — for dog roll

'We had to call in a bit of help with the nappies 'cos that's one thing I didn't have stocks of.'
— Michelle Carson, to RNZ, Nov 15

'We're trying to keep them close at the moment.'
— Michelle Carson, about her two children, to RNZ, Nov 15

The minor melee to sign up for the much-maligned second evacuation list is now beginning to ease. People who've put their names down head to the marae for breakfast. The queue stretches along the full side of the kitchen and dining room, outside but fortunately under cover from what's promising to be a scorching sun for this time of year. Kaumātua Major Timms emerges, looking at least as tired as he did the night before. He tells me the big water bladder they were expecting to be dropped off by chopper has not shown up.

We haven't the time to join the breakfast queue, but have heard that the supermarket is open again, so head that way in the ute. Beach Road was very quiet on the Monday, but this Tuesday morning a few cars and trucks are coming and going. The night before nothing had been open, but today businesses are stirring. There's a queue on the right at the BP station, opposite the Cod & Crayfish and Battery Town. A rough, handwritten sign on a piece of board propped up out the front carries a message about supplies being restricted to emergency services, so it's not clear to us why a line of everyday cars is snaking off the forecourt, or why a couple of cars are parked blocking the exit on the far side. For a moment, the gas station tableau calls to mind a scene out of *The Walking Dead* or another of those apocalyptic-zombie TV shows — although as this is New Zealand, there are no wild-eyed locals around and no guns.

A little further on, to the left, the front has fallen off the Mitre 10 store. The entire entry façade, 3 or 4 metres high and apparently a solid metre or so wide is lying face-down in the car park where it fell. Several people suggest to me that questions need to be asked about how this could happen to what is a fairly new building; similarly, Kaikōura's only shopping mall-type set-up, a fairly new cluster of buildings beside New World further up on the right, is damaged badly enough that two weeks later the businesses there still can't trade.

We're relieved to see quite a number of cars parked in front of the supermarket; we're less relieved to see the queue of 200 people waiting to get in. Local woman Sue Birnie is one. 'If you need something you've got to go and get it, don't yah?' she tells Tim Graham. 'So, just got to be patient … It's good that they're just letting six [shoppers] in at a time because it's your safety, in case there's another shake.' Tim asks Sue what she's after. 'Actually, a dog roll.' She laughs. 'Yeah, got to keep my animals.' Other than that, she has food in the freezer and a generator at home. 'I'm pretty well organised.'

Inside the supermarket, boxes, cans and bottles are piled randomly into masses of shopping trolleys parked so as to stop people heading down topsy-turvy aisles strewn with debris. A fellow shopper wants to get to the white bread that's at the bottom of a Pisa-style tower of plastic bread crates. A shop assistant and I lift them off so that she can get her ration of two loaves. What we really need is coffee, and toothbrushes and paste. We also pick up dehydrated food and baked beans, up to the maximum allowable limit of four of any one thing (two for bread), along with bottles of water and about a half a trolley full of chocolate, then head back out. The eftpos is offline but works in the end, and the cashiers are smiling — clearly tired, but smiling.

Someone else who is relieved is Michelle Carson — she is running out of supplies for their children Leo, three, and Isla, two. 'We had to call in a bit of help with the nappies 'cos that's one thing I didn't have stocks of, but luckily one of the girls I know managed to pop into the supermarket and salvage some for us … Keeping them fed is a bit tricky 'cos you don't have all your little bits and pieces that we would generally have in the cupboard for them, but they seem to be reasonably resilient anyway.'

She hasn't heard when the preschool might reopen. 'I know that the people who own it are up the Inland Road and they were hit reasonably hard as well, so whether they've got coverage I don't know — we usually hear from them mostly by email, so at this stage, no. We're trying to keep them close at the moment, and we probably need to get them into preschool at some stage eventually, but that's scary too, being apart from them.' Michelle works at the BNZ on the main street. No word from there, either. 'We're going to have to get back to work at some stage, so that's probably one of the big things.'

Andrew Penman in Nelson hears the reports about supplies dwindling, and he's worried. 'As soon as the road reopens, I'll be heading down there with some basics,' says Andrew. He's in the band Salmonella Dub, which has its recording studio base just north of Kaikōura. 'I know that everyone down there will be looking after each other and sticking together, and I wish them the best. I kind of wish I was there to help. I've got friends there that are out of supplies. From what I understand the town has been out of cash, out of petrol, food's rationed.'

The band's studio has escaped lightly. They built it on farmland negotiated from a farmer over a bottle of whisky 15 years ago. 'Of course, he considered it the worst bit of land on his dairy farm, but it was probably the nicest bit of land for us,' says Andrew. It turns out to be a reasonably solid bit of land, too. 'We're on the top terrace of the Hapuku Plain, right on the fault-line, and we seem to be okay. We're fortunate that we're on a rural property so we've got our own water and septic tank.'

Outside the Kaikōura New World, Melissa Hailes is loading up her SUV. She hasn't heard when the school at Hapuku, near the family farm, might reopen. Her two boys go there. She's queued and got in and out, grabbing the essentials. 'We only probably waited three-quarters of an hour, yeah, it's not too bad. They are doing really well, they are awesome in there, they are helping everyone with what they need, the staff are grabbing stuff from other aisles,' says Melissa. 'What did we get? Ah, toilet paper was the big one, stuff for the kids and things to keep them quiet, some marshmallows.' All 10 of the family are now living in the one undamaged house, with a second house not looking good.

The hottest of the hot-ticket items at the supermarket are a little surprising. 'While you'd expect water to be top of the list of must-buys post-quake,' says supermarket company Foodstuffs, 'it turns out that the most sought-after items are sweet, with over 3400 packets of lollies and chocolates sold in the first seven days post-earthquake.' Beer sales are strong, too.

———

The broken sheds

'We lost a little bit of stock down a crack that opened up and closed.'
— Henry Pinckney, farmer, to RNZ

'You can't just fix your house. That's the last thing that we need to fix right now.'
— George Murray, farmer, to RNZ

Melissa's mother-in-law, Rosalie Hailes, is helping her put the groceries in the car. They bought a big generator for their Hapuku dairy farm after the Canterbury quakes, and it's paying dividends. 'It can run the house, but it's not at this point … we are just living off a barbecue and what have you,' says Rosalie. 'That's fine, but the shed is the most important thing … So now we have the ability to milk, but [that] doesn't mean our milk's going to be collected … We will be tipping milk out unfortunately, and I have heard of farmers whose shed structures have been damaged so badly that they are going to dry their cows off.' She puts that number at three she knows of out of about 22 dairy farms in the district. They're also all having to check their irrigation systems in case the pipes have busted. 'We as a family are fine, it's the day-to-day running of the farm that's going to be a challenge.'

Hamish Bruce's milking shed is one of those that's wrecked. He's just put his heavily pregnant wife, Julia, on a chopper to Christchurch. When is the baby due? 'Three days,' he says. That's not the only drama: 'We have a one-and-a-half-year-old, too. The cot got broken in half with her still in it … but she's down in Christchurch now, so that's the main thing.'

They farm 460 cows on 160 hectares, 15 kilometres up the Inland Road. 'The farm in itself is not too bad, but the cowshed's basically a write-off. It's a rotary and it's basically broken in half. So we're just running them down to the neighbour's, milking them there once a day at the moment, doing what we can … From what I've talked to the other guys, there's basically us and another rotary that's stuffed and will need to be rebuilt, I'd say. Everything will be covered by insurance, it's just more an annoyance factor and trying to look after the cows and get water to them as best we can.'

Farmers rally round. Gore Town and Country Club holds a fund-raiser for sending cash north to run bulldozers to keep farm tracks open. Fire engines are used to get water to farms where troughs aren't refilling because of damaged pipes and tanks. 'They've been fantastic — they got all the way to the top of the hill in four-wheel-drives and took 10,000 litres up, which was almost impossible, I thought,' says Henry Pinckney, a sheep and beef farmer on the Inland Road near Wandle Downs. 'Some tracks are fairly stuffed and possibly won't be re-done. There are slips and you've just got to be careful of the safety for people. There's big cracks in the ground that could swallow a motorbike quite easily and you wouldn't see them.

'We've got cracks probably big enough to fit houses in in places, it's been quite phenomenal,' Henry tells RNZ's Alexa Cook. 'Unfortunately we lost a little bit of stock down a crack that opened up and closed, but we did manage to recover a couple as well — it could have been a lot worse.'

Cows are being shipped out. 'They got on a truck and went to Culverden,' a boy tells John Key when he visits Waiau School. Ian Thornton, our own neighbour in town at the house RNZ has rented, is a Canterbury farmer; he tells me how he's taken a bunch of cows to relieve the pressure. Rural insurance company FMG puts its share of claims at $40 million, and by early December has received 700 claims from 500 businesses.

Mark Hislop, who has two dairy farms, has been dumping milk for the past three weeks. 'Yes, a bit of a heartbreak,' he tells Alexa. 'It goes into the sewage pond and out onto the paddocks, and we've had to watch the spreading rates ... it can be quite tough on the pastures. We've got the irrigators going as fast as they can to spread it over as big an area as we can.' Tankers get through for the first time three weeks before Christmas. 'It's a big relief, actually,' says Mark. 'I just rang the area manager [of Fonterra] now and the tankers are actually in the community here and have started picking up milk.'

———

Tuesday, outside Kaikōura

'We can't get anywhere. So we have to juggle between a rockfall and a tsunami.'
— Belinda of Kaikōura Crayfish & Camp, to RNZ, Nov 16

RNZ's Simon Morton took to his mountain bike along the coast, and tells his story:

On Monday we made a call that I would try to hitch a ride on a helicopter down to Kaikōura and capture some

*stories of people outside the town and off the beaten track.
It would also be a chance to check up on some friends
living 30 kilometres north of the township, close to the
Ohau Point seal colony.*

*As high winds and biblical rains pounded Wellington on
Tuesday morning, I seriously wondered whether we'd
made the right decision. But thanks to GNS Science and
its rapid-response team, I got a ride south in a helicopter;
there was even room for my bike, a few kilos of muesli bars
and my camping kit. We flew to Omaka near Blenheim,
and then dropped some seismic equipment off at Seddon,
checking and installing more earthquake sensors on the
hills behind Kaikōura before I was dropped off at Black
Miller Stream with my friends, the Lidgards, that evening.
They had been due to celebrate their fiftieth birthdays
with a group of friends that weekend in Kaikōura, but with
no access north or south, the party was over!*

Simon started at sunrise on Wednesday at the seal colony and
waterfall at Ohau Stream, planning to go north through Okiwi
Bay to Waipapa Bay, detour west up the Clarence River Valley,
then ride onwards through Kēkerengū and into Ward along State
Highway 1.

*At Kaikōura Crayfish & Camp at Waipapa Bay, the owners
were in a horrible state of limbo. 'There's nowhere to go.
No matter which way we go, we can't get anywhere. So we*

have to juggle between a rockfall and a tsunami,' said the owner, Belinda. With the inside of their house trashed, they had keys in every vehicle ready to run if an earthquake or tsunami threatened. The couple had got a bank loan to stock up for the upcoming tourism season, which had just got under way. 'Our house is trashed and we've got nearly $20,000 worth of crayfish in the freezer just rotting, a couple of thousand dollars' worth of whitebait, 10 kilos of scallops.'

Up the road, an abandoned milk tanker stood with 20,000 litres of milk fermenting in it. Camper vans were left deserted along the shore, their occupants' food strewn in piles on the ground after they were evacuated. And the smell! The stink of thousands of decaying pāua and crayfish lying in the hot sun.

Simon heard of shearers who, with no work, loaded up their ute with tools and headed out to help people in any way they could. The families up the Clarence congregated on higher ground together, lighting a bonfire to raise their spirits.

Through Kēkerengū I pedalled, meeting Italian and Argentinian café workers who were now out of work ... For all of them, this had been an unforgettable experience.

Finally, exhausted after pedalling over 100 kilometres, it was getting dark and I needed to find a safe place to camp for the night. Entering the town of Ward I found the East Coast Inn, a hotel and pub, with its lights twinkling invitingly in the dusk. I just had to drop in. The owner had only bought the pub one month before, seeing it as a place to grow old in after a lifetime spent travelling around the world. Her plans for the future seemed to be dashed, but, incredibly, she is full of hope. It was one of the most moving things I had heard all day.

___

Better than Vegemite

'This morning our first aircraft just got airborne to assist.'

— Air Force wing commander Scott McKenzie, on RNZ *Morning Report*, Nov 16, 7.24am

'So we have people who get on beaming with smiles, and we have had others get on and burst into tears — I think just the relief of getting away from the aftershocks and of being trapped. Once they get off, we are dropping them to the Red Cross in Woodend School, and there's big smiles, big thumbs-up as they walk away from the helicopters.'

— Air Force wing commander Scott McKenzie, to RNZ *Morning Report*, Nov 16, 7.24am

By 10am on Tuesday, the first NH90 military choppers are doing their thing at the rugby ground behind the fire station off The Esplanade in Kaikōura. The blast from the blades is huge compared with the smaller machines; when one touches down, it sends a bag and a bicycle propped against a wall flying. Inside the clubrooms, under the board boasting of players' feats, people await their flight out.

> 'They are looking to get 16 NH90 helicopters flown out of here today with about 12 people per flight, so the operation is in full swing and a chopper is due to land in another 5 or 10 minutes here … Three flights today have left so far and they have got about four choppers doing the work.'
>
> — Tim Graham, live-cross to RNZ *Nine to Noon*, Nov 15, 10.56am

Megan Moffett of Wellington sits in a corner with her wife Rebecca Cathro and their two-year-old daughter. Megan looks utterly exhausted, but relaxed. The pressure is off. 'Being eight-and-a-half months' pregnant gets you to the top of the line quite quickly,' she laughs. 'No one wants me to have the baby here.' And not on the chopper, either? 'Yes, that would be preferable. We came for a family wedding and we were hoping it would be a simple trip.' As it is, they'll now be leaving their car behind, at the house of someone who offered. 'So [there's] a lot of goodwill going on,' says Rebecca.

Brothers Sean, aged nine, Tyler, four, and Ollie, two, are bouncing about the clubrooms like pinballs. Disrupted routines, chocolate and the prospect of a ride on a big grey helicopter can do this to a kid. Their mother, Becky Cresswell of Woodend, is looking only a little frazzled. 'They've been brilliant ... They actually slept through the 7.5. We didn't, obviously; it was very scary.' I ask Sean whether it was scary or exciting. 'Scary,' he says. John Cresswell says that they slept in the car as it felt safer than their beachfront motel. A bonus is that the chopper will land them in the playground of Sean's school in Woodend. What'll he tell his classmates? Sean mumbles something and goes back to playing with his brothers.

At one stage, an emergency call comes in from Goose Bay and a chopper is diverted to lift five people out: a couple of mothers with babies, an elderly person and a couple of children. 'The policewoman did a fantastic job on the beach ... they were very stoked,' says wing commander Scott McKenzie.

Parts of the rugby field evacuation are like being in a big-budget Michael Bay movie: multi-million-dollar, sleek new NH90s creating a grass-bending wash on the field; urgently scuttling air crews and soldiers in fatigues bearing medical supplies and escorting civilians; the type of defence-force-speak that defies reporting, all ETAs and FABs, whether from the air force or the navy the next day during the seaborne evacuation:

> *Navy:* 'We've just completed our side scan and our spot depth survey of the approaches and onto the wharf, so at this stage we are green for operations for the LCMs, but of course it is dependent on tide.'

Broken glass litters the streets in
central Wellington shortly after the
7.8 magnitude quake.
© RNZ / Rebekah Parsons-King

Tsunami warning sign on State
Highway 1 north of Blenheim.
© RNZ / Tracy Neal

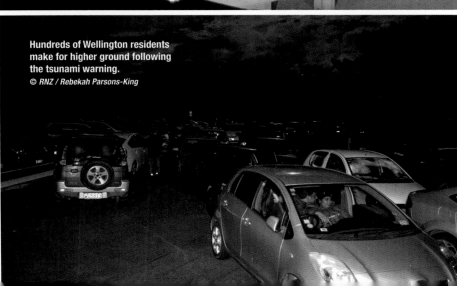

Hundreds of Wellington residents
make for higher ground following
the tsunami warning.
© RNZ / Rebekah Parsons-King

Fissures wide and deep enough to swallow a car wheel render the Inland Road impassable just east of Mt Lyford Lodge.
© RNZ / Rebekah Parsons-King

The Elms Homestead, where Louis Edgar was killed and his mother, Margaret, was rescued, is only recognisable as having been a home from the roofing iron that lies amid the masonry rubble.
© RNZ / Rebekah Parsons-King

Road damage on State Highway 1 north of Kaikōura.
© RNZ / Rebekah Parsons-King

Huge landslides overwhelm State Highway 1.
© RNZ / Rebekah Parsons-King

No way through – and the bill to restore the road and rail both sides of Kaikōura is put at up to $2 billion, though that's ballpark at best.
© RNZ / Rebekah Parsons-King

The railway line is torn free and tossed like a loose thread across State Highway 1 north of Kaikōura.
© RNZ / Rebekah Parsons-King

On Ward beach, the coastal rock shelf is raised by the force of the quake. Local fishermen estimate the rock shelf to be 2 metres higher.
© RNZ / Kate Newton

Severe road damage on State Highway 1 north of Kaikōura.
© RNZ / Rebekah Parsons-King

RNZ reporters Conan Young, left, and Patrick O'Meara get close to enormous boulders scattered over State Highway 1.
© RNZ / Rebekah Parsons-King

Buckled railing along a cliff edge on State Highway 1.
© RNZ / Rebekah Parsons-King

On a mercy mission from Gore to make sure his partner Lucy Millton's family is safe, Andrew Bowmar lands his Cessna on a safe stretch of State Highway 1.
© RNZ / Rebekah Parsons-King

Gary Melville's yellow-stickered home on Mount Fyffe Road, 4 kilometres out of Kaikōura.
© RNZ / Claire Eastham-Farrelly

The Melvilles cook on this makeshift barbecue for several days after the quake.
© RNZ / Claire Eastham-Farrelly

Chinese tourist Xiaodan Li is delighted to be airlifted from Kaikōura after the quake.
© RNZ / Rebekah Parsons-King

Mark Solomon and son Eddie, 15, beside the trench opened by the quake at their home on Mount Fyffe Road; they feel it's too unsafe for their extended family of 16 to return there.
© RNZ / Rebekah Parsons-King

Rakautara residents Tahua Solomon and Ngaio Te Ua will be stranded between two massive landslides for months.
© RNZ / Rebekah Parsons-King

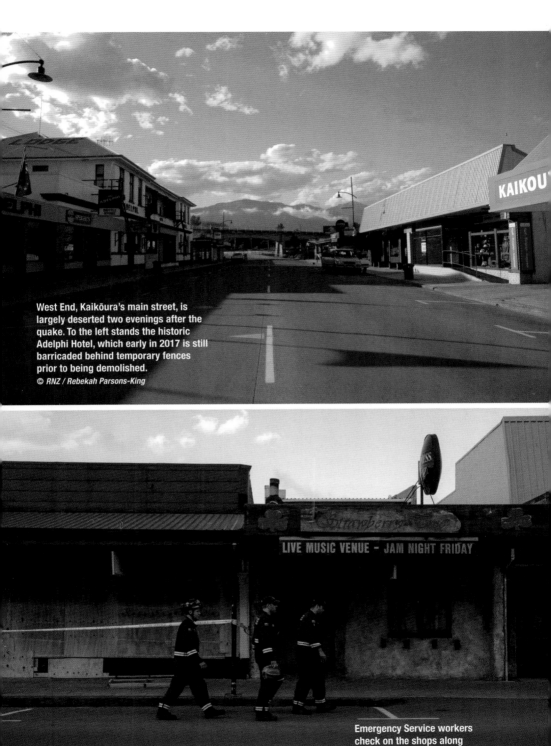

West End, Kaikōura's main street, is largely deserted two evenings after the quake. To the left stands the historic Adelphi Hotel, which early in 2017 is still barricaded behind temporary fences prior to being demolished.
© RNZ / Rebekah Parsons-King

Emergency Service workers check on the shops along Kaikōura's main road.
© RNZ / Rebekah Parsons-King

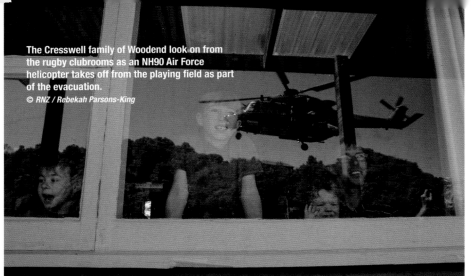

The Cresswell family of Woodend look on from the rugby clubrooms as an NH90 Air Force helicopter takes off from the playing field as part of the evacuation. © *RNZ / Rebekah Parsons-King*

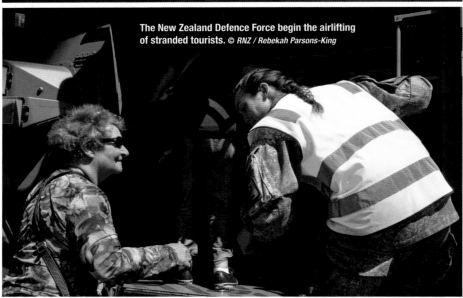

The New Zealand Defence Force begin the airlifting of stranded tourists. © *RNZ / Rebekah Parsons-King*

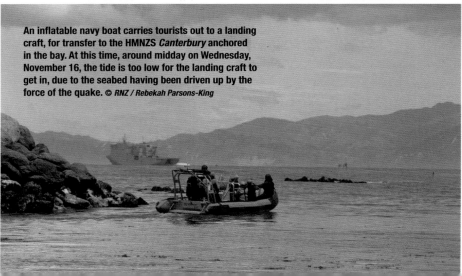

An inflatable navy boat carries tourists out to a landing craft, for transfer to the HMNZS *Canterbury* anchored in the bay. At this time, around midday on Wednesday, November 16, the tide is too low for the landing craft to get in, due to the seabed having been driven up by the force of the quake. © *RNZ / Rebekah Parsons-King*

Prime Minister John Key visiting Kaikōura on Wednesday, November 16, with a message that the government will provide financial aid.
© RNZ / Rebekah Parsons-King

Ex-All Black and Westpac mental health ambassador John Kirwan visits Kaikōura, telling people not to bottle up their feelings but to share them.
© RNZ / Rebekah Parsons-King

The Red Cross sets up a support centre at a primary school to help residents with supplies and mental health services.
©RNZ / Rebekah Parsons-King

Manager Kim Boyce-Campbell stands beside Kaikōura's only public swimming pool, which suffered significant damage in the quake and may be a write-off.
© RNZ / Rebekah Parsons-King

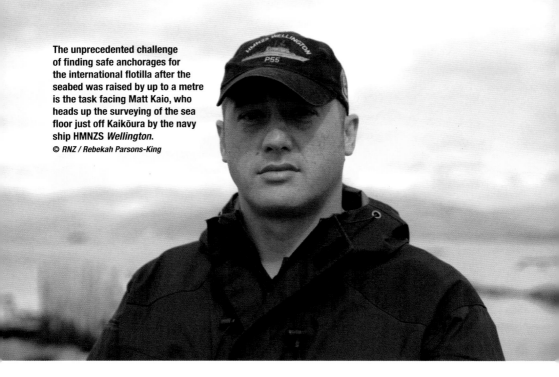

The unprecedented challenge of finding safe anchorages for the international flotilla after the seabed was raised by up to a metre is the task facing Matt Kaio, who heads up the surveying of the sea floor just off Kaikōura by the navy ship HMNZS *Wellington*.
© RNZ / Rebekah Parsons-King

A dam created by landslides leads to the evacuation of all residents in the Goose Bay community.
© RNZ / Rebekah Parsons-King

Water backs up behind a massive landslide on a North Canterbury farm; Rebekah Kelly's children wanted to call it Lake Quake, but she got in first and named it after herself.
© RNZ / Claire Eastham-Farrelly

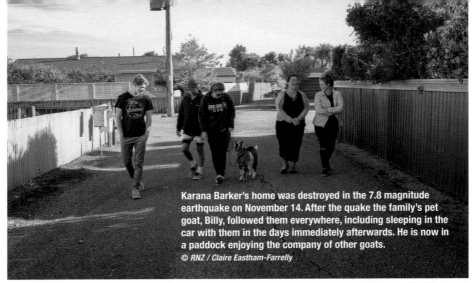

Karana Barker's home was destroyed in the 7.8 magnitude earthquake on November 14. After the quake the family's pet goat, Billy, followed them everywhere, including sleeping in the car with them in the days immediately afterwards. He is now in a paddock enjoying the company of other goats.
© RNZ / Claire Eastham-Farrelly

Billy the Goat is rarely tethered in normal times; instead, he prefers to walk around Kaikōura with the Barker family who rescued him.
© RNZ / Claire Eastham-Farrelly

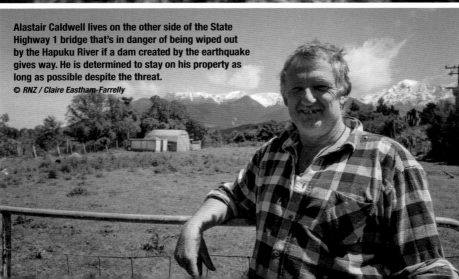

Alastair Caldwell lives on the other side of the State Highway 1 bridge that's in danger of being wiped out by the Hapuku River if a dam created by the earthquake gives way. He is determined to stay on his property as long as possible despite the threat.
© RNZ / Claire Eastham-Farrelly

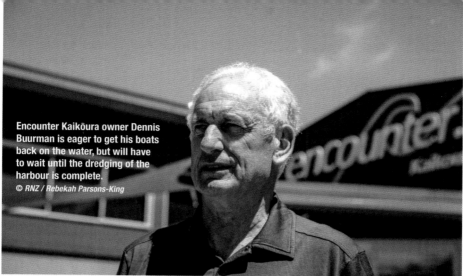

Encounter Kaikōura owner Dennis Buurman is eager to get his boats back on the water, but will have to wait until the dredging of the harbour is complete.
© RNZ / Rebekah Parsons-King

Kaikōura High School principal John Tait turns up to school to supervise the few students wanting to sit their NCEA exams.
© RNZ / Rebekah Parsons-King

Mike Vincent has travelled from Christchurch to relocate pāua that were dying due to the raising of the seabed.
© RNZ / Rebekah Parsons-King

Kids play as the first of the civilian convoys on the Inland Road awaits the green light.
© RNZ / Rebekah Parsons-King

It is feared that wildlife will have been scared away from the area by the sound of the quake. However, a week afterwards Encounter Kaikōura spots more than 300 dusky dolphins near Goose Bay.
© RNZ / Rebekah Parsons-King

RNZ: 'What's an LCM?'

Navy: 'Ah sorry, *Canterbury*'s landing craft.'
— New Zealand Navy officer Matt Kaio, to RNZ, Nov 16

Other parts of the operation are just delightfully un-gung-ho: evacuees scattered about the clubrooms' mix of second-hand chairs and tables; the certain knowledge that a cup of tea would be on hand if only the kitchen weren't trashed inside; the clubroom toilets which can best be described as from yesteryear; a few locals sitting on the plank-and-frame grandstanding enjoying the airshow.

Our team's contribution to this would be comic if it weren't so frustrating. We need to get our interview audio through to Wellington for *Midday Report*, but the rugby ground is a wi-fi blackspot. So we race up to the top of the chopper evacuation hill. Laptop open, I start sending the audio, in the blazing sun, without a hat, first crouched behind a Tekapo Helicopters ute and then beside a portable toilet next to a shipping container. I get one clip through smoothly, but the other one, of Silve Casanellas taking a swipe at our government, gets to 97 per cent and then fails. A second and a third attempt also fail; finally, at 11.59am the clip gets through to Wellington. I breathe a sigh of relief. Then *Midday Report* tells me, sorry, it was too late to slip it into the bulletin. They didn't use it.

Back at the rugby clubrooms, two septuagenarians from Brisbane, Jim Atkinson and Dick Parry, are sitting at a table with an elderly New Zealand man. They don't know him from Adam, but nevertheless he is helping them get sorted once they're off the chopper and beyond the disaster zone. 'Our friend Gray here, who we've only just met, has fixed us up with a car in Christchurch. He's also done the same for another fellow,' says Dick.

'We might get out of town and go somewhere quiet,' Jim says of the evening ahead. From there, though, rather than flee the country they'll carry on to Queenstown, aiming to walk the Grand Traverse. It is gratifying to realise that for many tourists this will have been a unique experience that goes far beyond sightseeing or whale watching; one that, the quake itself aside, they will not only never forget but will also have individual memories of — memories that can only do Kaikōura proud. Take Jim and Dick: 'Oh, the feed was tremendous,' Jim says. 'They put on 300 [kilos] of crayfish and we really all enjoyed it … I thought we'd get bread and butter and maybe a bit of Vegemite, [or] peanut paste.'

'The meals are certainly five-star,' says Dick. 'You know, as Bud says, I was expecting sandwiches and an orange perhaps, but every hour there seems to be a different meal coming out … a highlight of this, plus the warmth of the people of this town, they've been marvellous.' Not one person angry or upset, says Jim.

In the mid-afternoon we make time to get back to our rented house, boil some water and eat reconstituted dehydrated spaghetti bolognese while processing interviews from the evacuation centre clubrooms. The water is on, and the power, so RNZ picked the right street for us to stay in. But we still have no 4G connection from the dining-room table, so we drive back to the Cave Tours café near South Bay.

This time it's not deserted; the owners are there, cleaning up. Geoff Pacey is sweeping up the broken glass while he considers the prospect of picking up the pieces at PauaCo, a local company of which he is a director. He takes 5 minutes to consider whether talking to a reporter is something he really needs to do right now, then sits down with me. At the next table is his daughter, who can't get to her NCEA exams in Christchurch so will have to rely on her internals and mock exams. She's remarkably cheerful, as is Geoff for a guy with an awful lot on his plate and an entirely deserted State Highway 1 out the front of his large, low café set apart on its own just beyond the southern fringe of town.

'It's finished for summer already. It's been a very short summer,' Geoff says. 'No tourists, no business … Pretty hard on my staff, 'cos if no one's coming in the door I can't employ [anyone]. I think we have about 10 or 12 staff members. Same in the pāua industry. You know, until the roads are open we can't get the product in or out. So we've got Chinese New Year coming up … Ah, we do live exports here, so it's hard to get 'em out if we can't get them down the road to Christchurch.'

On a regular Tuesday afternoon it would normally be pretty busy here, with summer numbers beginning to build; now, 36 hours after the quake, Geoff could safely stand out in the middle of the highway for quite some time, and would only need to get out of the way of the odd car headed to the airport for a charter flight out or in. 'Absolutely not a truck in sight, not a car in sight, not a tourist in sight,' he says. 'There's more helicopters than anything in this town at the moment.

'Everybody's trying to come to grips with the earthquake. I'd love to keep my staff on in the café, and hopefully we can work something out, but, you know, if I've got no work for them I've got no work for them.' His other business, PauaCo, has a badly beaten-up building. They can't oxygenate their holding tanks, so are donating several hundred kilograms of shellfish to relief efforts. They're putting the word out to the 15 or so divers who supply them, who between them have a quota of 50 or 60 tonnes. 'They've gotta hold onto their fish until everything comes right, then we'll try and sell it somewhere else,' says Geoff. 'Can we get our roads open in five or six weeks? It's a bloody good question … What are we hoping for? Things back to normal, kids back to school, NCEA, things moving again.'

Geoff would offer us a coffee if he could, but there is no power on at his café. What he can do, he does — allowing Bex to leapfrog off the mobile hotspot in his car to try to send through her video. Tim, too, is having some luck getting his audio through. Soon, though, our time is up — we need to be back at today's pivotal spot, the rugby ground, for a live-cross into *Checkpoint* after 5pm.

'I'm here — you might hear the choppers in the background, I hope you can hear me … I think we have got one of those things that happens with disasters, John, sort of like a two-track thing: for the tourists there is some frustration and desperation, but for them it's a sprint back to normalcy — within a week they'll be out of here. But for Kaikōura locals, it's a bit of a marathon … What we have seen today is queues outside the New World supermarket — I've never seen that before — 200-strong queues just to get food … two loaves of bread, four bottles of water … The constant at the moment is these choppers coming in and out, but the irony there, John, is that the very tourists they are taking away are the lifeblood of Kaikōura, and I'm not sure what that means for the town …'

— Phil Pennington, to John Campbell on RNZ *Checkpoint*, Nov 15, 5.57pm

Another person in a chopper this Tuesday evening is Chessie Henry, daughter of Dr Chris Henry who helped with the Elms Homestead rescue. She is trying to get to her family, who are cut off up the Clarence River. 'When the earthquake hit early on Monday morning I was in Wellington,' she writes on RNZ's website The Wireless. 'I was scared, but I was also tired. I had work in the morning. I went back to sleep. Then I woke up to messages from my friends worried for my family. This was the first I'd heard of the quake being centred near my hometown …

'My dad, Chris, is a GP in Kaikōura, and was on call for the night when the earthquake hit, so he was staying in town. He has since been holed up there, completely consumed by the aftermath. Like so many other families, my mum, brother and cousin were stuck with no way for us to reach them, trapped in a horror-story version of our beloved home.

'Many of the families affected were completely isolated, unable to talk to anyone or have access to information about what had been going on … My family in Clarence had no idea where the quake had even been centred — my mother [was] left to helplessly wonder if the situation was actually worse in Wellington or Christchurch. She had children in both places.

'Sixteen hours after the first huge shake, Dad was finally able to phone me from Kaikōura. He had been able get to Clarence by diverting a [medical evacuation] trip on one of the Westpac rescue helicopters, and had been to the house for about 5 minutes before he had to leave again … Though the line was cutting in and out, I could hear — in snatches — Dad describing what he'd seen. All he could say about seeing Mum was that "everything she loves is broken". He also told me that our bridge over the river — the most solid and steadfast thing I can imagine — was completely gone. I asked if he meant cracked, perhaps? Unable to be driven over? "No," he said. "Gone."'

Chris tells Chessie to get on a plane from Wellington to Christchurch. 'When we were finally able to get a chopper in to get them on Tuesday evening, I was able to speak to them all for the first time,' Chessie writes. 'Mum described the four minutes of terror while the earthquake raged, paralysed on her bed with my cousin while our things smashed down around them. She told us how at night they lay together on the lounge floor, Mum in the middle with my brother Finn and cousin Hebe on either side ... The pergola that Finn had built with my father — and which we had excitedly watched our wisteria growing over for years — was now in pieces, some beams of wood now leaning ominously towards the house. We looked at pictures of the river, its course now changed completely, landslides marking the hills like scars. We realised, together, that we will probably never live in Clarence again.

'But somehow, something in all this makes me remember exactly what it is to be a New Zealander. I had no idea how much love I really had for the land around me until I saw it broken ... we will start again somewhere — and it will be in New Zealand, the land that has sheltered and protected us more than it has ever hurt us.'

Chris Henry will be flying here and there, fixing broken bones and tending to other injuries, for days yet, while his family are patching up what they can of their home. When I speak with him a few days later by phone in Oaro, where he's holding a medical clinic, he tells me the whole family has a deep connection and grounding to their Clarence home, so it's no surprise his daughter speaks of it so profoundly. His sons, though, are responding differently. 'I was laughing about boy brains and girl brains,' he says. 'She's written this incredibly emotional stuff and the boys are thinking, "When can we get the surfboards out?"'

—

The empty street

'Basically, the merry-go-round has stopped. And everybody's got off. And now we have to work out how to start the merry-go-round again ...'
— Kaikōura book-keeper John McDonald, to RNZ, Nov 30

Kaikōura, Tuesday, 6pm

From the rugby field near the seafront in Kaikōura, it is a short walk, and an even shorter drive, north to the main shopping street. On Monday, the dairy had been open. At tea-time on Tuesday when we walk down the street, virtually nothing is open — not the dairy, not The Whaler pub or any restaurants; only the district council offices for emergency briefings. The power is still out. As they say, it would actually be possible to shoot a rifle down the main street right now and not hit a seagull or a person, unless it was one of our news crew. Instead, Tim opts to do a walk-through for *Checkpoint*:

'Well, I can say I didn't much sleep overnight, John, because there were a fair few sizeable aftershocks last night and it was rough, I'm not gonna lie — but surely not nearly as rough as for the residents of Kaikōura who have damaged homes and businesses and are really just trying to kind of hold their nerve here … It's interesting actually, I'm on the main street of Kaikōura right now, just taking stock of the scene here. I'm outside the Four Square which is taped off with police emergency tape, there's newspapers from Sunday still on the rack in there, obviously, which haven't been moved, the "Closed" sign's up. I mean it doesn't get any more quintessentially Kiwi than that, does it really — the roped-off Four Square. And also here in Kaikōura, as I'm sure anyone who's been here will know, it's full of souvenir shops, and another real sign of the damage that's been done here and the shake that's been felt in so many ways is the pāua ear-rings that have been knocked over, it's the pāua necklaces, it's the key-rings, it's the mānuka honey which is jolted off its shelf in here, it's the cheese shop which is closed … It's a real picture of a small town that's gonna take a long time to rebuild.'

— Tim Graham, on RNZ Checkpoint, Nov 15, 6.35pm

———

Eddie and the barber's course

'We've got cracks probably big enough to fit houses in'

— RNZ headline, Nov 25

'The power supply is intermittent … in terms of the damage to lines, we were out Mount Fyffe Road … and there are power poles leaning wildly and there was one completely snapped on the side of the road; there are wires just running off into paddocks, into nowhere.'

— Phil Pennington, to RNZ, Nov 16, 7.20am

Tuesday, 8.30pm

Mark Solomon and the 15 people in his extended family, including his mum and his son, won't be going home. Their double-wing home on the worst-hit low-lying paddocks 4 kilometres northwest of Kaikōura has no services. It now has a 1-metre-wide, half-metre-deep trench running through the driveway and alongside the concrete slab foundation. Mark takes me there to have a look, with his 15-year-old son, Eddie. It's dusk; we have to hurry so Bex can film. Everywhere you go, though, it's a slow drive unless you want to skew your wheel alignment. The manhole covers on Mount Fyffe Road have popped up out of the asphalt by 20 centimetres. There's the occasional new judder bar or trench we have to brake for. Bex catches a very nice sunset looking towards the Seaward Kaikōuras, with a precariously leaning power pole centre-shot.

The picture at Mark's is not so nice. We hop over the trench and stand outside. Nothing has fallen down as such, but the longer we stand here, the more we realise it's all slightly askew. The two wings of the house have slumped fractionally lower than the main connecting kitchen that forms the bottom of the U. Consequently, the roof-line here is bending downwards, ever so slightly, on either side. On the south side, the concrete-block wall of Mark's mother's room shows signs of bowing — only a little, but it all adds up to a lot that is awry. From the air, we'd have thought that this house was fine; on the ground, it surely is not.

'That bow is because the building is pulling itself apart,' says Mark. He's a huge guy, tall and stout, with a gentle voice. 'That makes it a bit scary for your family to enter because we have got small children.' Six children live here, and three generations. 'I don't know if it's safe; we don't feel safe, but for the purposes of getting the message out we will just have a quick look — but if there's an earthquake, we are out of there.'

In the hallway, pictures hang at odd angles and cupboards have spilled all their contents out. Eddie's bedroom window is broken. The plaster between the walls and the ceiling is cracked. An antique organ — a family heirloom — survives, though the living room is in chaos. Mark's last memory of this room is of sitting in it watching TV. 'It started shaking and I thought, "Gee whiz, that's a big earthquake in Christchurch,"' he chuckles, 'and then the power went off and I thought, "Oh." And then about 2 seconds later it threw me across the floor and I hit the pot plant over here.' It's a distance of around 3 metres. 'I did try to stand up to run, but, oh, that's impossible ... My son come in and got me. They were all outside and he screamed out for me, looking for me.'

Eddie had run outside with some friends who'd been staying over. 'Oh, I wasn't going nowhere without my dad,' says Eddie, 'I had to get him.'

The communal kitchen we walk into next is the saddest space. It's awash with debris. Both big stainless fridges had fallen over. Structurally, it's hard to tell what's going on behind the linings. The family has a lot of stored memories of shared meals here. So has that all now come to an end? 'Oh, no; I think the physical scars remain,' says Mark, surveying the mess, 'but there's a [test of the strength] in the family unit when you come under these devastating conditions, and it makes you stronger, and you realise that the things that you thought you loved aren't as important as the family you have … We all loved our house because it enabled us to live together, but we love each other more.'

My cousin Marcus Solomon in Kaikōura. All our love
— Jeanette Horn, tweet

Un homme courageux
— Jacqueline Pantenier, tweet

Eddie shows us round the side to where the foundation slab appears to have shifted.

'There's a gap down in here which I can put my hand in between where the foundation was [and where it is now]. So you have got movement south–north of, who knows, three times the depth of my fingers; and on this side at least 120 millimetres, perhaps, it's shifted from east to west. Crikey.'

— Phil Pennington to mic, Nov 15, 9pm

I ask the teenager what his plans are now. Eddie says he'd signed up to do a barbering course in Christchurch, but that it depends on being able to go down there every month or so, and he's unsure how that will work out now. As for his friends, he expects they'll be hanging around Kaikōura. In his grandmother's wing of the house, framed photos of family groups hang crazily around walls that no longer form proper right-angles with the ceiling. They will need to get back in here to retrieve things like these photos that no insurance can cover.

For Mark, as for thousands of others, a big question is how Earthquake Commission and other claims will be worked out — and everyone is casting a wary eye at Christchurch's experience. 'Some of them have had okay experiences, but a lot of them have had bad experiences and a lot of them have had no settlement. It's taken a long time.' Mark rearranges his footing; he's straddling the trench that at this point passes through the grass just in front of his mother's sliding door. 'We're not a little family, we're three families in one; it's not what affects this family but what affects three families.' I ask him whether the land their home is on has any special significance as tūrangawaewae. 'It did, until it started cracking,' he laughs. 'The significance is that it was large enough for us to be able to see a proposition of all living together, but also a future; it was big enough to expand and become self-sufficient.' He and Eddie see no future for themselves here, in this spot, anymore.

———

The bishop and the supermoon

> '… these are hedged bets that get media air time due to the romantic misinterpretation that they were valid predictions.'
>
> — Professor in Tectonics and Geomorphology Mark Quigley, to *The Conversation*, Nov 14, 6.50pm

Tuesday, 9.30pm

On our drive back to town, the moon is up. It is huge and yellow and hangs off to the northeast, low in the sky, beautiful and slightly sinister at the same time. It's the middle one of a trifecta of supermoons in 2016, occurring when the Earth and the moon get closer to each other than usual. The sinister aspect is probably just a matter of hindsight; on Tuesday evening I haven't yet caught up with the theory that the supermoon's to blame for the quake. I'm appraised of this later by RNZ *Mediawatch*'s Colin Peacock, who tells how the story migrates from talkback radio to national and international news websites and TV over the course of Monday. He writes: '… with the ground still shaking, two people dead, hundreds of evacuees in limbo and the full scale of the devastation of the landscape still coming to light — why were national media outlets devoting all this attention to the issue?'

Nigel Grey, a member of a Facebook group dedicated to discussing weather modification, is being credited with an 'eerie prediction' that the forces of the moon being so close to the Earth could trigger a big tremor. This, and Destiny Church leader Brian Tamaki's suggestion in a rambling sermon on Sunday, just hours before the plates move, that sexual perversion and homosexuality prompt punishing earthquakes, receive a large amount of attention from some media, piggybacking on the 'gosh' factor so highly prized and purveyed by social media. Bishop Brian's defence looks like a backdown: 'The weather patterns have changed. Disasters are happening globally. Floods, storms, earthquakes. The seasons have changed and you don't need to be a scientist to understand this,' he says. Before it has gone 2am on Monday, a duty seismologist on one radio station gets asked about the supermoon. She sounds surprised at the question. Within hours there are online videos and articles about it.

The science isn't on either painting contractor Nigel or Bishop Brian's side. This fact is also spelt out in interviews with scientists, at least regarding the moon, but doesn't get quite the same amount of play as the claims. Professor Mark Quigley puts it in the category of fortune-telling: 'Deliberately vague predictions that provide no specific information about the precise location and magnitude of a future earthquake are not predictions at all. Rather, these are hedged bets that get media air time due to the romantic misinterpretation that they were valid predictions.' Yet, a full month after the quake, one news website has this: 'The November supermoon is famous for the Kaikōura earthquake, which happened on the same night ... and for the successful prediction from Weather Modification Watch NZ.'

The word in the park

'... you feel [the aftershocks] in the car, because the car bounces.'
— Sue Gray, to RNZ, Nov 15, 9pm

Bathed in the light of Tuesday's supermoon, RNZ's Tim Graham is at the hospital park talking to the tourists spending another night sleeping in their cars. Sue and Simon Gray are there. 'We're trying to get some sleep now,' she says. 'We are hoping to go up to the centre tomorrow morning to find out whether we will get over on the ship. We know it's on its way 'cos of our daughter in the UK who's been looking up all the details for us online, that we can't get at the moment, so we know it's on its way from Auckland ... We saw it in Auckland when we visited a week or so ago.' They've been told that the military choppers would only take people with small bags. 'We have a case each, it's not a huge case each, but we said, well, we'll wait for the ship and let other people go.'

'There were priority cases, too,' says Simon, 'older people and people with illnesses and things, so I think it was right … We're happy to wait.' They say that communications are patchy and the update in the park at 1pm that afternoon by a Civil Defence person was fairly unhelpful for them; but then again, it's aimed at the locals. 'And, of course, we've got to appreciate the locals are in a dire situation. They want to know about roads and water,' says Sue.

They've got a hotel room but aren't staying there. 'Because of all the tremors we're still getting we don't like being down there,' Sue says. 'The shaking of the actual room and building is worse than being in a car … You feel them in the car, because the car bounces, but at least we know nothing's going to fall down on us.' Tim mentions to them how a Dutch man on the other side of the park has just told him the same thing, but then Tim had pointed out a power pole he hadn't seen.

The car does have its drawbacks. 'It's just getting a little bit sweaty,' says Sue. 'We're not able to wash because of the lack of water; we understand the problems they've got there. So we're just grinning and bearing it, and [will] hopefully get a wash in an airport somewhere.'

'It was a shocking experience for us and we're both quite on edge now,' says Simon. 'We just woke up to sounds of crashing — glasses and crockery were just smashing onto the floor violent shaking of the room. We could just feel the building swaying very violently and we were both scared ... it was a terrifying experience.'

Friendly Texan Stephanie Wang has left The Albatross hostel for good for a tent in the park — 'This is the new Albatross,' she jokes with friends there. She has her own car and has her hopes set on the Inland Road being open soon. She's unstinting in her praise of the response. 'Really, the community has just pulled together in an incredible way. I mean, we all have each other's backs. I mean locals who have power and who had water ... they were cooking food and giving away food for free.'

It's another late night for us sending through our audio to the newsroom. For Bex, it's worse still as her video comes in bigger digital packets. She doesn't get back to the house until 2am.

———

The bunker

'Taking stock in the shaky capital'
— RNZ, Facebook, Nov 14, 6.14pm

'I have nothing. Absolutely nothing.'
— Toby Jones, Wellington apartment dweller, to RNZ

Wellington, Monday and Tuesday

No one in central New Zealand is immune from the quake, including Prime Minister John Key, who, although an Auckland electorate MP, lives in Wellington during the weeks that Parliament is sitting. He comes on RNZ's *Morning Report* before embarking on a chopper flight to survey the damage around Marlborough and Kaikōura.

Kim Hill: 'How are you?'

John Key: 'Well, I think like everyone, just a little bit shaken. I mean the ninth floor of the Beehive here, where my office is, it must have been really moving, because there's just broken glass, crockery, televisions, computers — everything's just gone south here in a major way. I thought Premier House was shaking, but it must have been nothing like the impact up on the ninth floor.'

Kim: 'Did you not have Blu-tack under everything?'

John: 'No, obviously not, no.'
— RNZ *Morning Report*, Nov 14, 8.02am

While the prime minister's crockery was flying about on the ninth floor of the Beehive, the lights were flickering on in the bunker in the basement at the National Crisis Management Centre. The centre is understated —more like the Kaikōura rugby clubrooms than the White House Situation Room. It does, however, have cabin-style bunk-beds, food, fresh sheets and a lot of the latest communications gear. None of it is stuff you would want to get wet. Early on Monday, it is flooded with people; on Tuesday, it is flooded for real when a water pipe bursts during a debilitating rainstorm in Wellington. It's a sufficiently embarrassing incident to be aired during Parliament's Question Time on Thursday afternoon, but is ultimately played down as a damp squib that doesn't compromise the country's disaster response hub.

From where I sit in sun-soaked Kaikōura on Tuesday, it does seem cruel that in the capital a flood has been heaped on top of a quake. On Monday's *Morning Report*, Guyon Espiner had said that gale-force winds and torrential rain were due to hit Wellington later that day. 'So when are the locusts arriving?' his co-presenter Kim Hill drawled. I know that wild weather's hit the centre of the country and the Hutt River is in flood. I also know that the stopbanks are high, and that the street I live in is okay. I find out that, although the quake has put paid to NCEA exams for some, my son has made it through the downpour to Hutt High to tackle his physics paper.

Wellington's new mayor, Justin Lester, declares the central city open for business from Tuesday morning. Commuters, already jumpy from the shaking, now have to cope with shocking visibility on the roads and stormwater up over their hub caps. The drive back out to the Hutt Valley in the afternoon is a nightmare: a choice of 4-hour snarl-ups to go 13 kilometres along State

Highway 2, or clay-slide after clay-slide on the alternative route around the Pauatahanui inlet. There's a log-jam, too, in RNZ's Wellington office, and every other newsroom in the country, as they try to scramble reporters and producers to cover a minor disaster popping up inside a major one.

The sun will come out again; and it does, throwing into starker relief a problem that's not going away any time soon: the growing collection of Wellington buildings compromised by the quake. White and red tape warning 'NZ Fire Service: Authorised Entry Only', flapping in the wind, becomes a common sight cutting across footpaths in the central city. Structural engineering reports trickle in from early on Monday, and first one, then half a dozen, then 50 buildings are cordoned off.

'QUAKE LATEST — Police close Wellington's Molesworth St over building safety concerns'
— RNZ, headline, Nov 15, 5.07pm

When the cordons are later relaxed, 16 multi-storey buildings remain evacuated and closed; some old, some new, some for good, but most temporarily. Among them are Farmers Trading Company in Cuba Street, NZ Post House on Waterloo Quay, and the Defence HQ. At 61 Molesworth Street near Parliament, where a structural beam is found to have fractured like a bone, closure is immediate. The building was empty anyway, apart from a Filipino family and a few other tenants who had been allowed to live there illegally. Demolition starts quickly, live-streamed. In contrast, at the shiny Asteron Centre opposite the railway station thousands of IRD workers are allowed back in, and it's only days later that further checks throw up questions about the stairwell and lead to a temporary shutdown.

People whose homes are in cordoned-off buildings have it tougher. Mary McIntyre lives opposite the parking building at the Reading Cinema complex. Shortly after the quake, she's told to quickly pack a bag and leave. 'Luckily my niece was coming in through the door; they didn't know anyone was living there.' Toby Jones can't get back in to his apartment nearby. 'I have nothing. Absolutely nothing. I just came from work, so I have my work clothes on, and a phone with half a battery. That's it,' he tells RNZ's Mei Heron. He only arrived from England a few months ago. ' It was the first earthquake I've ever experienced, so I didn't know what to do … I was in the shower at the time actually, and I kind of stumbled out of the shower and fell to the ground, put some clothes on, didn't dry myself at all, and ran into the living room under the table.'

> 'LATEST: Large Wellington CBD block — around
> Courtenay Central — shut over quake risk'
> — RNZ, headline, Nov 17, 4.25pm

> 'QUAKE LATEST: Ten buildings in central city
> evacuated, dozens of people affected'
> — RNZ, headline, Nov 17, 4.46pm

About 200 people are evacuated from buildings around the cinema car park. In mid-December, more than 100 residents of the Maison Cabriole apartments on one corner are given just 20 minutes to go back in to get their belongings out, with help from firefighters. Brittany Godderidge rescues her two-year-old goldfish, Sir Swimsalot. 'He hasn't been fed for a month, but he's still alive,' she tells RNZ's Michael Cropp. His tank is gross. 'It was green and slimy and smelly, so that's a big cleaning job now. When we first got evacuated we only got told it was going to be two days, so we grabbed small things for only two days, and then the next day we were told two weeks, and then it was four weeks. Now it's an extra three months.'

> Hells bells Sunday earthquakes cannot be the norm.
> Sitting at the table writing & suddenly everything is
> swaying. Apartment life sucks. #eqnz
> — Jodi Ihaka, tweet

The BNZ building on the wharf looks like it will also be out of action for months; rumours circulate that the near-new Statistics House nearby will have to be pulled down. This is another headache for the building's owner, CentrePort, whose wharves have ruptured. 'There has been a situation where the floor sections of the building have separated away from the beams of the building,' says port chair Lachie Johnstone. 'This has happened in isolated areas of the building, and I really need to reiterate how fortunate we were that this occurred overnight.' Elsewhere on the wharves there are cracks and buckling, and liquefaction closes the container terminal. Photos show containers stacked in a slightly precarious Jenga style. In the long-term, some buildings may be moved off the waterfront. While this is no Christchurch-type scenario of a city needing to be re-created in large parts, still Wellington has been changed by the Kaikōura quake; it will end up looking different because of it.

The government announces an inquiry into how buildings in the capital performed, with a focus on Statistics House; shortly afterwards, a financial aid package is released. Shonagh MacLeod of Thorndon's Word of Mouth café and catering business, which is out of bounds behind a cordon, is frustrated in her efforts to get help. 'As soon as we were locked out, basically our café income stopped,' she says. In mid-December, the city council — using the emergency earthquake powers just given to it by the government — orders the owners of 80 buildings to get more detailed and invasive engineers' inspections done by February 10. Up its sleeve it holds the legal power to enforce this order if building owners don't comply. There are commonalities among the 80: they are 4 to 16 storeys high, and are made of reinforced concrete with precast concrete slab floors. Buildings included are Bowen House, opposite Parliament, The Treasury building at 3 The Terrace, the Intercontinental Hotel and the Wellington Public Library.

The list of confirmed casualties grows to encompass a cinema complex and car park at the region's biggest shopping mall in Lower Hutt; demolition begins in early December. A supermarket opposite remains cordoned off, as does the restaurant and bar at the Angus Inn where the manager is wondering how to cope with a big wedding function. At the Reading Cinema car park off Courtenay Place, a work colleague's car remains quarantined; she can't get it out, or get an insurance payment until demolition starts.

A tenant exiled from an adjoining building, photographer Lance Lawson, talks of having to pay rent even though his office is off-limits, probably until at least March 2017. Next, he gets a phone call — 'out of the blue from somebody I had never met before'. It's someone called Dennis, Lance tells RNZ's Eric Frykberg. 'A lovely man, and he said, "Look, I have got three empty spaces of varying size and I heard about your plight and it should not happen to anyone. So if you need some space just yell out and you can have it free for as long as required." I was just blown away, it was a wonderful gesture.' On top of that, the owners of a local café offer him spare warehouse space, again at no charge. 'It is wonderful, human nature; it is brilliant.'

People in a place like Wellington really have no choice but to look out for each other in ways like this. There's no resisting these sort of forces on your own; one-man-bands are all very well, but they do best in a gentler place than this. Frankly, though, you do have to be mad to live in a city where shocking weather is guaranteed and catastrophic quakes are inevitable. The November 15 flood is simply the icing on a relentlessly revolting spring in the capital. Did anyone ask John Key whether the real reason he quit early in December was to escape the shakes on the ninth floor and the leaks in the bunker?

4

WEDNESDAY:
EXODUS BY SEA

'Key in Kaikoura: "The whole mountain has moved."
Prime Minister John Key has arrived in Kaikoura for his
second visit to the town since the massive earthquake
on early Monday morning, as relief efforts arrive in
force ...'

— RNZ, Facebook, Nov 16, 11.53am

Never thought I'd be so pleased to see the US navy
arrive!

— Joy Danford, tweet

Olympic hopes

'Even though this is pretty heart-breaking, my big
hope is that ... we can get together as a community
and really focus on getting a new pool.'

— Kim Boyce-Campbell, to RNZ

Kaikōura's district council offices are buzzing with emergency
services people at 6.30am on Wednesday. Public relations people
are among those being flown in to relieve the wrung-out staff
on the ground. Men and women in army and navy uniforms
stride purposefully around. The mayor, Winston Gray, helpfully
gives Tim and me a quick update on where services are at before
Morning Report calls up for the early live-cross:

'Good morning, Susie. I'm up in the Kaikōura District
Council building looking out the window at a calm,
clear day. A lot of activity in behind me with police, with
Defence, and they are just having a briefing now ... I
think there was a sense of a vice in operation, giving a
bit of a squeeze-on with the water going out for much
of the town. But now, hearing that there's this response,
these foreign ships are coming in and also the [water]
drop by the Hercules ... [and] the council is saying they
are doing a lot of work, they have got piping in from
Cheviot ... On Mount Fyffe Road, which is the main
pipe that goes up towards the hills; they are going to
be doing big repairs along there. They are saying that

it is possible that they will get good, clean bore water
— and a lot of it — down that pipe by this afternoon,
and that they will be able to get it to most of the town,
if not all of the town … A few people have some water,
some residents probably in the higher streets, and the
council has a list of those and they are actually advising
residents who really need water that they can go to these
people, and they have arranged for those people to
share their water, so that's really good to hear as well.

'Winston Gray said he's not unduly concerned about
the sewage … The medical officer of health had
said that now's the critical time … Mark Solomon,
just anecdotally, he said that the stream — the little
creek out on Mount Fyffe Road — that there's a smell
of sewage, that he's seen it leaking into the stream
and that he saw someone with dreadlocks who was
getting washed yesterday and he had to warn them
that there was sewage in that stream.'
— Phil Pennington, on RNZ *Morning Report*, Nov 16, 7.20am

Heading out of the council building, Tim and I come across Tony
Robson and Jo Thorne. Tony got power back on early on Tuesday,
but lost his water later in the day. 'And sewage, we've been told
not to actually flush anything or put anything down the drains
since basically as soon as it happened,' says Tony. 'So we're
all using portaloos and conserving as much water as possible.
I've got a bathful of water just at this moment, in time to, like,

give out if anyone needs it … We'll be able to last as long as we need to, really. Ultimately, yeah, it's the sewage thing I think is probably the big thing that's gonna cause most problems.'

Jo's come down to volunteer after spending the previous day helping people clean up. 'I thought, "Well, what else can I do to help?"' She lives down on Torquay Street opposite the cracked community swimming pool. 'There's no water down there, the water switched off straight away,' she says. 'There's no sewerage down there either, so it's peeing outside and trotting down to a portaloo.' Naturally, some of the 48 portable toilets dropped strategically around the town are getting a bit full; certainly that's the case with the only one I can spot while down at South Bay later on Wednesday. The cavalry arrives on Saturday: trucks bearing 900 chemical toilets, one per household.

'The water, we just ran out this morning, just trying to refill our containers,' says Jo. 'There's somebody up there says somebody's got an artesian well and we can go fill up from that … so my partner's just gone off to try to sort that one out … We have only got one 40-litre container maybe, yeah, that's it, but that lasted us three days. You can conserve quite well. We've got a rain barrel that we've been using to wash the hands and … dishes and things.

'I've got a barrel sitting under my drainpipe — so's Tony, I think.' Tony nods, and Jo carries on, 'So we've got barrels from school that we've taken down to use as water gatherers … we've put a sock over the end of ours to filter the chunky bits out, and then we've got a filter at home as well that we've used overseas, so we'll be putting it through that. And then you boil it. You can manage.'

There'll be no such jury-rig for the 46-year-old Lions Pool, though. It was on the verge of opening for the summer season; now it's a write-off. 'It's been through many violent storms and each time we patch it up and carry on, but this is a bit of a death blow,' pool manager Kim Boyce-Campbell tells RNZ's Ian Telfer. 'Even though this is pretty heart-breaking, my big hope is that … we can get together as a community and really focus on getting a new pool.' Chris Elson hopes so, too. His job as one of five pool lifeguards is now gone, and he doesn't want to also lose his edge as a competitive swimmer. He has set his sights on the 2020 Olympics. Without the pool, he's feeling a bit twitchy and really needing a swim. 'It doesn't have to be anything fancy. Just a 25-metre pool, indoors, that's it, and it would make a whole lot of difference to the town.'

The thousand kindnesses being done every hour under this state of emergency certainly prove that little things can make a big difference. It's also true, though, that big things can make a bigger difference. For the tourists intent on sprinting back to their regular lives, it's a big deal when we hear — courtesy of Winston Gray from on top of the evacuation hill where he takes a call from *Morning Report* at 8am while surveying the ocean — that the naval ship *Canterbury* is now in the bay below. The seaborne evacuation is at hand. At the same time, the prime minister is flying down in a chopper on his second visit, this one a big deal for the district's 740 businesses.

> They are isolated. I do hope the US sends our friends
> to the South some assistance
>
> — American Greg Johnson, Facebook

We miss the arrival of the ship, having dashed back to our house for breakfast; we had been expecting the *Canterbury* to arrive after 9am. The search for a square meal, which led us to stories on Monday night, has let us down this time. It underscores the hit-and-miss nature of reporting in a disaster zone. Everyone we come across — even the officials — has only part of the picture. Some of the information we get is entirely wrong. We're gathering eyewitness accounts, but people's own memories of what happened, and when, get jostled. There's very little ability to cross-check what we're hearing without badgering our producers in Wellington or Auckland. There's no asking Google: we have no internet most of the time, and no time to check details when we can get it. We still don't have a map.

It gets a little embarrassing when ABC Radio in Australia calls during breakfast wanting a quick live interview. Like any good producer, the ABC guy checks out what I can cover — and the very first thing he asks has me stumped: 'Can you tell us about the cows?' 'What cows?' I reply. A chance to be a foreign correspondent, and I've muffed it. This is when, via an Australian broadcaster, I learn about the Kaikōura quake story that's captured more headlines and social media space globally than any other: the story of the stranded cows. As I listen to the producer, I realise how close we were to reporting this story ourselves — it's about Andrew Bowmar, the Gore farmer whose Cessna we came across parked on the highway near Clarence.

The family of Andrew's partner, Lucy Millton, farm Waipapa Station, on the southern bank of the Clarence River, 30 minutes north of Kaikōura. After the quake hits, her first thought is to get to them. Andrew tells RNZ that he needed no convincing — the choice was easy.

The couple fire up their Cessna 185 in Gore and are in the air by 8am. Landing isn't easy. Unable to talk to anyone at the farm, and unsure whether the grass airstrip has been damaged in the quake, Andrew circles trying to attract attention. It works. Clarence River Rafting's Ben Judge notices the plane repeatedly buzzing his base. 'Andrew and I didn't talk at all, but I could see him circling and knew what he was up to.' Ben gets some of his workers to stand at either end of a section of the highway, indicating a safe place for the plane to land. 'There was a tonne of room because there is a parking area just there where people get off,' Andrew says.

Saved ... but next stop meatworks
— Hayden Rule, tweet

This is where Tim, Bex and I spotted the plane on Monday morning. Later that day, Andrew takes to the air again to check up-river for the rafting party. Meanwhile, a chopper flying a *Newshub* crew over the family farm spots and takes photos of two heifers and a calf stranded on a knob of grass jutting up 5 metres or so, a tiny piece of hillside paddock left behind when masses of the rest slid away. It's extraordinary that the beasts weren't buried in the landslide below. Andrew posts the pictures online, and the cow story goes viral. An Auckland artist makes a picture out of it. Animal rights group PETA Australia chimes in: 'PETA is calling on the farmer to let these cows live out the rest of their lives in peace.' The cows are mustered off the knob, a little anti-climactically as it turns out — they simply walk down the back side of it. Farmer Derek Milton vows they won't be sent to the works.

> 'The cows left stranded on a quake-created island near Kaikōura have been brought to safety ...'
> — *Newshub*, tweet, Nov 15, 11.02am

———

The prime minister and the craypot

> 'It's kinda hard.'
> — local businessman Dennis Buurman, to RNZ

> 'We'd laid in bed this morning thinking about that, what we're gonna do, 'cos Kim could lose her job as well.'
> — Mike Becconsall, to RNZ

Wednesday brings a double-down for the news team; Tim goes high and I go low. He and Bex head up the hill to catch

John Key's visit, dropping me at the marina with the HMNZS *Canterbury* out in South Bay. There's a palpable mix of goodwill and uncertainty at The Craypot Café and Bar, where two dozen or so business leaders gather to meet the prime minister under the craypots hanging from the ceiling. The place wasn't open the night before, or on Monday, but it is now. There is a lot of hand-shaking, a lot of back-clapping, a lot of 'John this' and 'John that', and hardly a negative word or a sceptical aside. The PM is in his element; it's never more important than when the fabric's stretched to ripping point by trauma to have that political skill he has in spades: showing he's 'one of us'.

'Prime Minister John Key has come here to, as you say, reassure business owners as they enter peak season here. Many of them are very worried at a business leaders' meeting this morning. He's told them the government is going to help them, throw money at this, to get them through the tough times so they can retain staff and their businesses in the long run. But he said it's too soon to announce details of that just yet, he's planning to do so tomorrow, he hopes … Business owners say they would've liked to hear a few more concrete details today, but they understand that these things take time to pull together. The prime minister is saying it's going to be a package similar to the one structured for businesses after the Christchurch earthquake, so it's just taking time to get the ducks in a row.'

— Tim Graham, live-cross to RNZ *Midday Report*, 12.01pm

John Key's motto is similar to that of Takahanga Marae: 'I'm here to help.' He contrasts his flying visit on Monday with today's. 'You can certainly feel that there's a lot of momentum, people are feeling a lot better and a lot stronger and can see the support that's pouring in,' he says. 'As soon as we can get the roads up and running, the connectivity working, then ultimately new tourists will be able to come into town. So it's a combination of [businesses] having the confidence they can keep their staff and bringing tourists back when infrastructure can support that … It's totally a tourist-dependent town, so if we can get the messages out there quite quickly, that it's up and running and operational again, then we can sort of stem that real risk for Kaikōura. If we don't do that quickly, one of the concerns is that people take it off the list of places they're gonna go because they think it's a no-go zone.' John Key suggests using Richie McCaw on social media.

Dwayne Fussell, who owns Coastal Sports, has a think about what the PM has said and suggests that it won't be enough to get the town through this. He says the new reality is of Kaikōura being 'isolated on an island'. 'If you don't make [money] through the December, January months, you're not here the following summer. The house, the mortgage, the business — everything is on the line.'

Daniel Jenkins thinks that his business, Kaikōura Cheese, whose shop on the main street looks largely undamaged but is closed that first week, could go bankrupt. His family has gone from the heights of being featured on *Country Calendar* on TV in October, to this nadir. In the meeting he pushes John Key for specifics, suggesting that if support is not adequate then businesses may be forced to relocate for a year, and look to shift back after that.

One reporter's question brings the wider issues of the day to bear, and reminds us of the upset result in the US presidential election just days before; it seems like an age ago. John Key confirms that he had a phone conversation with US President-elect Donald Trump that morning. 'He offered his condolences and support for the people of New Zealand, obviously the people most directly affected here in Kaikōura.'

> '... you're not a good luck charm then.'
> — John Key, to a tourist, Nov 16

John Key then heads up to the marae. A Perth couple tell him it's been memorable — they're also on their honeymoon. 'Oh, your honeymoon!' says the PM. 'Oh, well done ... You'll get out today, we'll get you out, it's all good.' A Scotsman tells him that Kaikōura is 'like Scotland on steroids'. Europeans, Americans, Asian tourists, Australians, Kiwi tourists, locals — he carries on, shaking hands: *You'll be fine, okay, it's all good, they'll sort you out*, over and over.

An Oregon couple mention how they didn't talk to their embassy — 'We didn't even think about it' — and that now they're heading to friends in Christchurch. 'You'll be swapping earthquake stories,' jokes John Key, adding, 'We're not quite as earthquake-prone as it sounds!' A New Zealand woman tells him how it's the second time her family's had a reunion, and the first one coincided with them being in Christchurch for the 2011 quake there. 'Goodness gracious me … you're not a good luck charm then,' he responds.

Dennis Buurman, the owner of one of the town's biggest businesses, Encounter Kaikōura, is buoyed by the prime minister's flying visit, which begins and ends at the rugby ground helipad inside an hour and a half. Yet the next day, when the government lays out its $7 million relief package, his business is excluded. There's also a $350,000 package for Hanmer Springs, which has escaped with little structural damage but is suffering a downturn in visitors. The Hanmer Springs Forest Camp Trust has a bunch of schools cancel their camps. Parents are worried about sending their children to a quake-hit region, according to manager Elizabeth Meaclem. 'Even this week we're three schools down,' she says in early December. 'Next week we're a couple of schools down. Schools have still made an early decision to cancel camps the week of the earthquakes, even though they weren't coming until this week or the next.'

For Kaikōura, an eight-week subsidy is introduced — but only if you have 20 or fewer staff. Dennis Buurman has 50 or so. Bigger businesses like his get the carrot of more tailored help, but they don't know quite what yet, and the uncertainty is eating into the ability of people to hold their nerve. 'We were just into full swing,' Dennis tells RNZ at the end of the first week. 'It's kinda hard,' he adds, struggling to hold back tears. He's just told his staff that the prospects for work are not looking bright.

There's a desperate urge in this small town to remain upbeat about the few baskets that all their eggs are in. A day or two earlier, Dennis had been feeling better: 'At least we know the wildlife is still there, so, once the road is open and we can get the boats out, we'll be raring to go,' he says. Three weeks on, though, only 150 or so vehicles are travelling into the town each day, with another 150 leaving by convoy on the Inland Road. It's like being on a mad metronome, feeling hopeful one minute, despondent the next. So Dave Stanford is cautious about putting his view out there. 'I don't want to be the wet blanket of Kaikōura tourism,' he says, then goes on to tell me that he thinks it's too early to encourage tourists to come back. This in late November from the owner of two backpackers', including The Lazy Shag which just two months before got YHA status. He cancels all his bookings in December and January — those that haven't already cancelled themselves — and means to wait it out.

'If you didn't get to take a shower day after day, and you were down washing in the sea like I was … I can see the summer slipping away, but let's not be too quick,' Dave tells *Morning Report*. The strain on the resources is one thing, the lack of viable attractions another. Dave twice goes out around the seal colony walk around the peninsula, and ends up holding his nose. 'When I walked around there last night, you go under the cliffs [and] you have to run past bits because you think, "Hey, there's going to be an aftershock", you know. You see where all the debris has fallen down, the putrid pools full of dead limpets, dead kelp and, you know, is this the side of Kaikōura we want people to come in and look at?

'Let's get the place cleaned up and operating normally, not like a back-country camping ground.' Dave puts on a fairground busker's voice: 'If you want to come and see a rock slide, this is the place, mate. Just come up and we'll show you where the mountain used to be and where it is now.'

Dolphin Lodge owner Helen Blanchard is also taking a cautious approach. She says that the temporary halt she's called to operating might become permanent. It's just too hard to decide at this point.

Employees control their own fate still less, at least when it comes to staying in Kaikōura, though their ability to up sticks is greater than for employers. Michael Becconsall works for PauaCo. He's lived in Kaikōura for half a dozen years. 'I heard from the employer, they said don't panic, you know, we're still getting paid and, you know, don't get worried. They've been good.' This is on Wednesday morning. But he's realistic. 'I think it's going to be pretty hard. I work in the pāua industry and I just cannot see that surviving through this, so I just don't know what will happen there … We specialise in exporting live pāua so there'll be none of that for ages, I imagine, so there'd just be no work.' What else could he do? 'Not much in Kaikōura, Kaikōura was always a hard town to find work anyway … I don't know — we laid in bed this morning thinking about that, what we're gonna do.' He laughs, and points out that his partner, Kim Sheppard, will probably lose her job as well. 'You know, tourism's not flash.'

Kim has been in town only a month. 'I just work in a tourism shop … selling merch and, you know, clothing … So, no buses, no people staying in Kaikōura, no clothing getting sold. That's quite big and five months there, yeah, that's their time to make the money.' She smiles ruefully at the timing: why this couldn't all have happened in April when the shops were going into their winter hibernation, instead of November? 'It would've been perfect timing.'

Like a number of others we talk to, Kim also went through the Canterbury quakes. 'I had a nasty experience in the February one, so I'm a bit nervy again, because this one was even more substantial … Yeah, I'll be glad when the aftershocks stop.' It wasn't that she was a quake refugee; coming to Kaikōura was a considered move, although that's now having to be reconsidered much sooner than she could have anticipated, taking into account things like trying to sell a house. 'I think that will recover eventually; you just have to ride through it all. It'll become more of a specialised area to come to, maybe, than just any old tourist town. Maybe it'll be more for people that like fishing and boating and like the Marlborough Sounds, places like that.'

There are plenty of jobs in town, of a kind. Government departments have sent in people, such as Education Ministry staffers to help restart the schools. Contractors of all kinds, especially roading and telecoms, are on deck. Many are being rotated in and out by chopper or small plane, as are the RNZ news crews, though later on I meet a data-cable contractor in the Pot Belly Café who has been in town for 17 days straight. Kathy Christian at the Gateway Motor Lodge says she's chocker with emergency services and health board workers, and the same goes for the Bella Vista and the Lobster Inn. The TVNZ crews are spending a bit of cash down at The Whaler pub most nights. 'Some of them are sort of slowing down now. Once they've done their thing they'll head back home, and what happens after that I'm not sure,' says Kathy. 'We've had hundreds and hundreds of cancellations for the next couple of months.'

I am surprised by the number of business owners I talk to who have only just set up in or bought into the Kaikōura economy. Kathy Christian swapped life in Timaru for the 4.5-star Gateway four months before the quake; Steve Blume had just a two-week buffer of normalcy after buying Dive Kaikōura off veteran operator Nigel Elson; Mike Toni's in the middle of rebranding Bad Jelly Backpackers after taking over this year; and I hear of a fish-and-chippie who had left Havelock after a fire at his shop there, to get his fryers going in Kaikōura — he had three days' grace before he was out of the frying pan and into another kind of fire.

New business owners were drawn in by optimism and market buoyancy. Nearly everyone mentions what a great season they were expecting, in many cases after a cracker one last summer. Now it's a case of hanging on and surviving. 'There was great excitement and anticipation that it was going to be a good season,' Lynette Buurman, co-owner of Encounter Kaikōura and the town's tourism convenor, tells RNZ's Patrick O'Meara. 'People had taken on lots of staff, we'd invested in infrastructure, a new boat, we were going ahead with confidence. So this is just the worst possible thing that could happen. And we are now facing a year or two before we can really say we're through this.'

There's no more apt metaphor than that provided by the Whale Watch Kaikōura boats. The seabed has risen half a metre in South Bay, and at low tide the four big catamarans now sit on the bottom. Each day they have a very narrow window of 3 hours of high enough water to get out and get back in. Normally Ngāi Tahu would be running a dozen tours a day, ramping up to 16 a day over summer. Three weeks on from the quake, Kaikōura's biggest tourist attraction is not operating at all, while engineers explore options for dredging the seabed. 'Our former low tide is now our high tide. And the low tide is like nothing we've ever seen before,' Whale Watch's general manager Kauahi Ngapora tells John Key and Gerry Brownlee when they tour the district in early December. 'This marina is like a hub — there's probably about 30 boats that use this, that rely on this harbour to be open, for them to get out and make a living out on the ocean.' The government announces that it will change the law to get the marina dredged faster, as well as to allow landslip debris to be dumped directly into the sea.

It will take all this, and more, to refloat the tourism industry here. Meanwhile, the catamarans rise and fall on the tide, held in their berths behind a big rock seawall. The businesses themselves have less protection than the boats, and what buoyancy there is for them comes by way of the government aid package — which later is extended into March 2017. After that, they might be back flat on the bottom. Tourists are the tide, and the tide is out.

———

The South Bay show

'We won't forget Kaikōura.'
— Frenchwoman Louisa, to RNZ

'*Canterbury* arrived zero-hundred this morning. We got pushed by helo from the ship … We've set up a lifejacket point for tourists to rotate through there.'
— staff sergeant Simon Haughey, Nov 16, 9am

If the air force can put on a show at the rugby ground, the navy can do so at the bay. Most of the time the big grey ships do their real work far out of sight of regular taxpayers, on fishing patrols or cyclone relief in the Pacific, or applying military diplomacy in the Gulf. When on occasion they do come into the likes of Wellington harbour, it's almost always for some commemoration or other — officers and crew are in their dress uniforms, polished and precise and possibly not all that useful. Here, I can sense the obvious relish with which the navy people are rolling up the sleeves of their regular fatigues to get stuck in, at home, off a boat-ramp and a skinny pier under a brilliant sky in intimidating circumstances. 'Normally we travel with military personnel,' says staff sergeant Simon Haughey, who's the beach master today. 'However, we have trained for this, and we have moved large numbers of civilians in scenarios like this before ... We're trained for this, we do do this a lot.'

> 'HMNZS *Canterbury* is right in front of me in South
> Bay, and a chopper is flying in from it and the
> *Wellington*, which has been doing some surveying
> to make sure they can get in; so that arrived about
> 8.30. [The chopper has] already dropped two loads of
> lifejackets, in 1500-kilo bags ... It flies across the bay
> from the boat ... comes in with a bag on an angle out
> behind it on the line and is dropping them ... about
> 5 metres from me.'
> — Phil Pennington, to RNZ *Nine to Noon*, Nov 16, 9.07am

An unprecedentedly curly one, however, has confronted Matt Kaio, the commanding officer of HMNZS *Wellington*. The seabed has shifted. They can't just barrel in relying on the charts from November 13. The surveying curve-balls are not just hitting the navy, either: Land Information New Zealand puts out an advisory to say it is working with GNS and Otago University to collect survey data at key markers, and meanwhile it's best to be cautious about determining whether the quake has altered boundaries. Matt Kaio says it's looking promising for South Bay, although they're dependent on the tide for how many people they can move. 'At this stage, because the tides are so low and the seabed has moved slightly, it's given us less margin and clearance for the keels; so what's happening, we'll transfer people in and out by [inflatable boat] and once the [landing craft], which can take approximately 100 people, is full, they'll take it out to the main ship.'

We're standing on the boat ramp. There's no danger of getting in the way of the fishing boats today; they're all parked up behind us on huge trailers. The underground fuel tanks below the boats are locked tight behind a keypad that requires an internet signal to run, and there is none. McKeown Petroleum is working on getting them unlocked; Ken McKeown tells me that they supply the whole fishing fleet, so the lack of fuel, and the new look to the seabed, are big obstacles in the way of getting that industry going again.

Matt Kaio says that his ship's next move is to survey north of the peninsula before the other naval ships, including the USS *Sampson*, the Canadian frigate HMCS *Vancouver* and the Australian frigate HMAS *Darwin*, arrive overnight. Locals 'reckon it's moved [up] a metre on the other side, so yeah, we'll confirm that in the next 24 hours … The weather's about to change in the next 24 hours, so we need to work, find some landing points; and that's my job this afternoon, to find some landing points on the northern end of the peninsula.'

And regarding naval commemorations, I may have been premature in questioning how useful they are. 'What actually happened is the New Zealand Navy, we've been celebrating our seventy-fifth birthday and we've had all these foreign warships turn up to help us celebrate — and lo and behold, there was an earthquake, so [we] just had a lot of ships and a lot of capability there and … why wouldn't yuh? Yep, may as well have one now when there's a lot of ships about.' Matt chuckles. 'However, we're actually due to head down to the Southern Ocean, to Antarctica, to conduct a patrol down there.'

> '… there are no tourists here at the moment …
> just some bemused locals. People are out on their
> verandas, there's a chap on a bicycle in a high-viz vest
> and he's watching, and another couple of guys in their
> gumboots, and there's us.'
> — Phil Pennington to RNZ, *Nine to Noon*, 9.07am

Three neighbours are sitting on a bench looking out over the marina and the mini-armada of grey naval inflatables, each manned by four crew all in black, motoring their way in from the *Canterbury*. 'We've never been able to see all those rocks exposed. Even at extremely low tides, you'd see a bit, but not to the extent out here,' says Peter Duncan, who lives in South Bay. And it's not even full low tide yet. 'I'm retired up here. But what it does mean is the tourist industry's going to suffer very badly … It might be a couple of years, this effect, because people don't like coming to earthquake-prone areas.'

By 10am the inflatables are tied at the pier. A half-hour later, the first bus full of tourists rolls in. The army and navy both have people here, and a couple of crew off the orange Coastguard boat are helping too, along with four men who have been crawling over the decks of the Whale Watch catamarans. One of them tells me they were ready to go at 7.30 this morning, the plan being to use the big cats to rip on out to the *Canterbury*. Their size and speed would have made it easy to transfer all the people. He doesn't know what's held things up, but they're now out of time and tide. Perhaps it's just as well: the irony of Whale Watch only getting to use its boats to take the tourists away for good might just have been a bit too bitter.

> 'We have got three Zodiacs tied up at the wharf. We
> have had the first bus — they are using the Whale
> Watch buses — [it] has just pulled up with tourists on
> board. They are going to get along the pier onto those
> Zodiacs, and then out to a landing craft halfway out
> into South Bay, and then on to the *Canterbury* from
> there. They had been hoping to use the Whale Watch
> boats, the big catamarans — four of them, massive
> things — but because the seabed has risen half a
> metre, the tide is now too low and very shortly those
> boats will be on the bottom.'
>
> — Phil Pennington, to RNZ news bulletin, Nov 16, 11am

Charlie Smith and Megan Roberts are among those first off the bus. 'Relieved to get off, get away, that's it, just want to get home,' Megan says. The couple have been working down in Queenstown. A one-night stopover at her sister's in Kaikōura on the way to Auckland turned into a couple of nights in a tent in the front yard — 'up high'. Charlie takes a different tack. 'I'm lovin' it, yeah. Beautiful day, mate,' he says. I ask him whether, like me, he's almost getting used to the aftershocks — the smaller of them anyway — like being on a rollercoaster long enough for your adrenaline to dial itself back and your heartbeat to settle down, simply because it's impossible to stay amped up for too long. He nods, though for him it's trickier: 'I get a bit of sort of motion sickness.' He points out to the *Canterbury*, 'I get seasick anyway, so *that* should be fun.'

A group of four Spanish tourists is a lot more animated. 'We hope this is the time for us to leave,' smiles Luis Grau. 'We're going to get on that ship, big ship, and get to Christchurch. It's going to take long time, like 9 hours I think,' says Joan Ayala. Does he get seasick? 'No.'

'I do,' says Nuria Pascual, 'but I have my pills with me. I bought it for the whale watching but I couldn't go, so I hope now is the time to use it.' None of the four managed to go whale watching. 'But maybe now we can watch some whale [on the *Canterbury*],' laughs Nuria. Asked whether the holiday's been all bad, Joan says it's all about perspective: while they are still in Kaikōura, they still have some risk, 'but as soon as we get to Spain it will be good experience, yeah'.

A couple of naval crew in blue coveralls are getting lifejackets out of big white bags and fitting them to people. 'Everyone listen up,' says one. 'To inflate the lifejacket all you need to do is you need to pull them out and the lifejacket will inflate … If you go into the water, the lifejacket will inflate automatically. So no problems there. 'Kay, so once we tuck in our loose straps that should be us good to go … Sir, could you take the first team over there, please?'

The first group of 10 head for the Zodiac. It includes Sam Helm and his brother Dan from the UK. 'Yeah, very good, can't wait,' says Sam. 'It's not been too bad, they looked after us very well … You get treated better here, don't you? … But glad to get going.' An elderly American man in cargo pants has a spring in his step. 'Really happy, oh, it's great to be going … The night of the shake, that was really nerve-wracking, but since then it's been good.'

The evacuation goes smoothly:

> 'It is proceeding apace; in fact, we must be on Zodiac number 10 with 10 people on board, making 100 people who've been ferried out to the landing craft. The orange boat of the Coastguard has also been taking people. They've had two busloads of tourists so far come on … I would say at this rate they're going to be able to head off to Lyttelton some time early this afternoon, and that's going to be a return run to do supplies back into the bay.'
>
> — Phil Pennington, live-cross to *Midday Report*, Nov 16, 12.03pm

It takes until maybe five o'clock for all of the tourists to be safely carried over to the *Canterbury*. Later in the day, as the tide rises, the Whale Watch catamarans are able to help and the naval landing craft *LC02* is able to get in to the pier. They're taking a few more folk than they had earlier suggested: not 250, which is a regular contingent, but more like 455 plus 4 dogs and 7 tonnes of baggage. Ultimately, the *Canterbury* will evacuate a total of 640 people, 9.3 tonnes of baggage, a cat, 17 dogs — and about 30,000 bees. Its commanding officer, Simon Rooke, later tells TVNZ: 'One of the evacuees just could not leave his bees behind. I smiled when I read the cargo manifest just before we sailed. It is the type of entry you'd probably see if they did an inventory of what went into Noah's Ark.'

It's an 8-hour trip down to Lyttelton, where the passengers will get off and loads of supplies will get put on. It's not quite what young Frenchwomen Lucie and Louisa had in mind when they were picking a holiday. Initially, they had been desperate to fly home straight after the earthquake. But now, standing on the deck of the landing craft in their lifejackets, picking up a tan in the bright sunshine, they reappraise things. 'We just wanted to leave as quickly as possible, but now we're okay and we're going to continue our trip around the South Island,' Louisa tells RNZ's Max Towle. 'But we won't forget Kaikōura.'

One evacuee, Ivo from the Netherlands, says that the rescue effort reminds him of Dunkirk, where hundreds of thousands of

Allied troops were rescued from the French beach during World War II. This sparks some heat online.

> It was the look of the craft they were in, I'm sure, no disrespect intended
> — Pat Taylor, tweet

A day and a half has passed since tourists were writing their names on lists outside the marae, and some were venting their frustrations about the evacuation to us. By the next morning, RNZ newsreader Nicola Wright is able to sum it up: 'The military evacuation of hundreds of tourists and locals from Kaikōura is over. The operation began with the air force's NH90 helicopters carrying people to Christchurch and ended last night with evacuees being ferried out to the naval ship *Canterbury*, bound for Lyttelton.'

Bex, Tim and I spend our last 2 hours in Kaikōura in the marina car park, hunched over our laptops trying to send material through. The bright sun makes it impossible to see the screen if the laptop is on the bonnet, so I end up putting it on the driver's seat and kneeling on the road, the sun beating down on the back of my head. At 3pm we head up to the evacuation hill, and an hour later we have swapped with an incoming three-person crew and are on our way home. Pretty soon we are all crashed out in the chopper; once again, I miss the chance to ask whether we can set down at the overlooked Clarence farms.

5

AFTER WEDNESDAY:
THE LONG ROAD TO RECOVERY

'It looks like a big, huge ploughshare has just gone
screaming across the landscape from as far as we
can see in one direction to as far as we can see in the
other direction.'

— GNS senior scientist Russ Van Dissen, to RNZ's Tracy Neal,
Dec 1

'It's not going to be the same as it ever was, as the
seabed has risen that much.'

— charter fisherman Mark Sanford, Kaikōura

'Miraculously, Gary's preserves have all remained
upright'

— Conan Young, RNZ reporter, Nov 18

The scientist and the ploughshare

@gnsscience seismologists flew over Kaikōura today.
They told @alexperro they've never seen the earth
move so much

— RNZ's Alex Perrottet, tweet, Nov 14

This is how the November 14 earthquake is described on the
GNS website:

Public ID	201p858000
Intensity	Severe
Depth	15km
Magnitude	7.8
Location	15km northeast of Culverden
Type	earthquake

This is how it was experienced on the ground:

'The most terrifying night of my life.'

— Amy Cook, tourist from Reading, UK, in Kaikōura, to RNZ

'Just the noise and really violent shaking.'

— Sarah Black, Hanmer Springs, to RNZ

To appreciate the enormous power unleashed by such an
earthquake, you need only to look out of Jacqui Hamilton's
window over the land stretching 10 kilometres down the

Clarence River valley towards the sea. With a photo to hand, you can compare what you see now with what there used to be, on November 13. 'The bridge is lying in the river, yes,' says Jacqui, who raised her children here for 21 years and now lives alone on a 4-hectare block. 'We had a lot of uplift and a lot of land damage up the valley. Apparently, we live on a fault line and that fault line ruptured … I was talking to one of the geologists, and she said the fault that ran under our houses was only a fault they *suspected* was there.

'It is totally surreal: you go to bed at night and the landscape is as you've known it for 21 years — and the next morning it's changed out of sight.' She laughs. The difference? 'Oh, I can actually see the Clarence now. I couldn't see the Clarence before 'cos it was running low. So I'm higher. My land was all flat and now it's undulating and fractured; it's got terraces everywhere, my garden's all full of terraces and great big splits. Some parts of the land have come up, some parts have gone down, and at the Clarence itself, it's a lake rather than a flowing river. I mean it's still flowing, but there's a great pool of water there … about 6 kilometres back up the river.'

Every earthquake is unique, but the Kaikōura one is off the charts for its complexity and the puzzles that it's now presenting to a whole raft of scientists. They need to unravel its secrets, to understand more about why and how the Earth moves — and when it might happen again. On GeoNet's website, a map of the top of the South Island lets you watch the rupture march up the east coast as it triggers seismic sensors first at Hanmer Springs, then at Kaikōura, then Molesworth, Kēkerengū, Ward, Seddon. Some of these sensors had been rolled out across Canterbury and Marlborough only since 2010, in a $45 million GNS–Earthquake Commission programme aimed at placing 30 new seismic stations and 16 GPS sites in the Marlborough fault zone.

One minute and one second in, it's recorded as only a 6.5 magnitude — 'only', though the wrecking ball that was the February 2011 Christchurch quake was just 6.3, but shallow and located right under the city. Two minutes on from the initial hit, the recorded magnitude rises to 7. It's not until Wednesday evening, just after 6pm, that enough data have been crunched from both the sensors close at hand and those more distant to declare the quake a 7.8 — which means it has released 89 times more energy than a 6.5.

A geological shuffle of this magnitude leaves its mark. From space, Japanese and European radar satellites that measure the distance to the ground incredibly accurately, and so can spot any shifts, confirm that the quake has caused massive permanent displacement of the land in the northern half of the South Island. NASA releases images from its Earth Observatory that show new land thrusting out into the sea. The biggest shifts are across the Hope and Kēkerengū, and the Hundalee and Papatea faults. To the east of these faults, the land has shifted mostly southwest; to the west, it's moved mostly northeast.

GNS computer simulations suggest that at some points on the Kēkerengū Fault north of Kaikōura, the land has done a radical, 10-metre sideways slide either side of the fault-line. It shifted in just a few seconds. Clarence farmer Julia says they heard the water being tossed sideways out of their concrete swimming pool, and at the same time it was like going upwards, quickly, in a lift. She's been told that they were subjected to 3Gs of force. What's more, according to GeoNet, this is one of the most complex earthquakes ever observed, in the same league as the 1855 Wairarapa earthquake and the catastrophic 1906 San Francisco earthquake that travelled over hundreds of kilometres of the San Andreas Fault. One puzzle is why the Hope Fault, which links the Alpine Fault to the ones that ruptured, has hardly moved at all.

The mysteries of fault-lines are myriad. GNS senior scientist Russ Van Dissen knows this much, although he also knows the Kēkerengū Fault better than most. He takes RNZ reporter Tracy Neal on a tour of the land around the fault. At one point he stands inside a chasm twice his height, pulled apart on a farm near Ward. 'It looks like a big, huge ploughshare has just gone screaming across the landscape from as far as we can see in one direction to as far as we can see in the other direction,' he says. 'It's not often you see a fault that ruptures by up to 10 metres. Fissures in the ground are common, but the size of *these* are uncommon because this displacement is way bigger than common.' At another spot, the split dirt crack of the fault sweeps unbroken around a small hillside, like a thick trail of oil left on a banked race-track.

Initially, it's thought that six faults ruptured at 12.02am, with a combined jolt equivalent, some say, to 400 atomic bombs. Then the number goes to seven, and by early December GNS has updated this to 10, including the Fidget Fault and the newly named Uwerau Fault. While the appreciation of what's occurred is immediate — right before my eyes as I fly over State Highway 1 near Clarence on Monday morning — the understanding comes gradually, in fits and starts, as the experts drill down through the evidence. 'This particular rupture has let the cat out of the bag in some respects, because it's ruptured a series of faults that we wouldn't have thought would rupture together in an earthquake of this magnitude,' GNS's Jamie Howarth tells Tracy Neal. 'That has implications for how we go about modelling seismic hazard in this country.'

Russ Van Dissen sees it as confirming a theory they'd been working on. 'When we pieced the story together and actually got the results back, we identified three big ruptures in the last 1200 years. So in the last thousand-ish years, this fault has ruptured three times — and now it's the fourth time. Four hundred years sounds like a long time to humans, but as far as the fault-lines go it's one of the most active in New Zealand.'

The way the sea has behaved carries its own mysteries. Many people have wondered out loud whether Civil Defence was crying wolf with its tsunami alert. No way, according to Helen Jack, a geological hazard analyst at GNS: 'The earthquake triggered a tsunami, and if it hadn't been for the substantial coastal uplift in many places, and the low tide at the time, it could have been much more damaging,' she says in a blog post. 'Currently the only report of the tsunami impacting property was at Little Pigeon Bay on Banks Peninsula, where a house was badly damaged. However, there are numerous reports of the sea leaving seaweed, shellfish and fish stranded above high-tide level. There are also observations of the sea level falling below low tide, rising and falling quickly, and strange surges and currents.'

———

Sea life, and death

'There are hundreds of them here having a good time
— I think they're happy to see us.'
— Rachel Wilkerson, dolphin tour guide, to RNZ

Back in Kaikōura, the mass of tourists has now gone. The odd one or two hold out, counting on the Inland Road opening so they don't have to leave their car or camper van behind. But mostly the tourists, and their tourist dollars, have left — and when will they be back? It can be depressing to think ahead. For locals, the first sighting of a pod of whales off the coast, on November 20, lifts morale. 'Great seeing our Tohora today. 5 in total at the end,' Whale Watch tweets.

Three days later, Encounter Kaikōura spots more than 300 dusky dolphins south of Goose Bay, alleviating concerns that they might have been scared off. RNZ's Alison Ballance writes that if ever there's a time to let most marine animals off lightly, then mid-November is it — though not for the pāua and crayfish baking in the sun on the uplifted rocks. 'As a rough guide, the bigger the animal, the better off they were,' she notes.

Spring is a quiet time for whales at Kaikōura, and out in the offshore canyon a few sperm whales and perhaps some beaked whales would have been feeding and resting. Large pods of dusky dolphins would also have been offshore before November 14, with two resident pods of little Hector's dolphins closer to the land. New Zealand fur seals are close to giving birth in breeding colonies on rocky shore platforms, including at the large Ohau Point sanctuary. Up at a waterfall pool here, where the seals congregate, the quake brought down large slips and the pool is now full of rocks. But it happened just *before* they were due to give birth; good timing again. Albatrosses, petrels and shearwaters, red-billed gulls and little penguins were safely out at sea doing their thing.

A lot of people told us about the noise of the earthquake on land. 'It would have been even louder and more terrifying in the sea,' writes Alison Ballance. 'Undersea earthquakes are the loudest event in the ocean, and a magnitude 4 earthquake is on record as reaching 272 decibels. And sound travels faster and further in water than it does on land. The sound of the 2011 undersea earthquake off the coast of Japan, which caused a devastating tsunami, was recorded on underwater microphones on the coast of Alaska, hundreds of kilometres away.' NIWA acoustic loggers will have caught the sound of the Kaikōura quake.

'Sperm whales and beaked whales don't like loud noise at all,' Professor Liz Slooten, from the University of Otago, tells RNZ. So they'd have swum a long way away, very quickly. The Whale Watch sighting, thankfully, shows that at least some have returned. The Hector's dolphins, though, are more inclined to become disoriented.

Gary Melville, who drives boats for Albatross Encounter, says that the big birds are just as numerous now. 'I'm sure they probably might not even have noticed.' As for the seals, a ranger reports seeing hundreds of fur seal pups, just one or two days old, born 100 or so metres north of Ohau Point.

For one species of small bird, though, it's bad news. Rock slides have filled the Kowhai River valley to a depth of 70 to 80 metres deep in places, burying the burrows of Hutton's shearwaters. A hundred thousand pairs of birds normally breed there, and there are slips, too, at Shearwater Stream, where they also breed. Apart from these birds, however, most wildlife appears to have got off lightly.

It's less clear what's happened to life on the seabed. The Kaikōura Canyon is one of the richest deep-sea habitats in the world, full of burrowing sea cucumbers, spoon worms, bristle worms and irregular urchins, and supports big populations of fish —

including rattail, hoki and orange roughy. Large numbers of massive submarine landslides triggered by the earthquakes have set off a flow of waterborne sand, mud and water, hundreds of metres thick. It's travelling down the 60-kilometre-long Kaikōura Canyon and hundreds of kilometres north into the Hikurangi Trench, burying seabed life as it goes.

The flow of debris extends at least 300 kilometres from Kaikōura. 'It is still settling on the seabed from the water column,' NIWA's Dr Philip Barnes tells Alison Ballance. But big quakes are part of the cycle here, measured over millennia, and a rebound is certain.

The confounded crayfish

'This is home for me, I grew up in the bay, and all this reef is just dying now.'
— Heath Melville, to RNZ

At the shore edge, the immediate devastation is gut-wrenching — literally, given the smell of dying pāua and crayfish shortly after the earthquake. PauaCo director Geoff Pacey is watching a video on his phone, sent to him by one of his contract pāua divers 36 hours after the 7.8, at an outside table at the Cave Tours café that he also runs. 'Wow, look at this,' he says. It shows exposed rocks covered with pāua drying and dying in the sun. I ask if we can post the video on the RNZ website. No, says Geoff, do that and hundreds of people will descend looking for a free feed. I agree not to. In hindsight it was a ridiculous decision. Few people could get near these rocks, or at least would attempt to try in these circumstances. The greatest uplift, and the most exposed shellfish, are as you go further north towards Ward, where the biggest slips are.

Dire early estimates are that up to three-quarters of the pāua and possibly a bit less of the crayfish along the coast will end up perishing. Like many other figures bandied about in such uncharted territory, it's a punt. 'It's not going to be the same as it ever was, as the seabed has risen that much,' says charter fisherman Mark Sanford. 'Kaikōura is known as the home of pāua and crayfish, but it's not going to be like that again for, I'd say, 10 years.'

Primary Industries Minister Nathan Guy is alarmed at the prospect of the entire fishery collapsing. He imposes a one-month closure of the $23 million crayfish harvest, and three months for the $1.5 million pāua fishery and on seaweed gathering, until scientists can get a better handle on just what has happened here. Yet by mid-December, it's announced that the rock lobster fishery ban is being lifted because a review's found that stocks have not been severely reduced. Biology, geology, seismology — rarely has such a fascinating event occurred when our scientific tools are advanced enough to have a real poke at it. It's a once-in-a-lifetime opportunity that doubles as a once-in-a-lifetime — you hope — curse.

The chair of Te Rūnanga o Kaikōura, Henare Manawatu, is happy with the fishery ban, even if it lasts a year. 'We think it's a good idea, shutting it down — we're quite prepared to accept it with the understanding that if we have a tangi or a special occasion we can issue permits for divers to go and get our kaimoana under our cultural take.' The local pāua industry associations have by this stage imposed a voluntary ban on commercial harvesting, but note that some people are just going out and helping themselves. It's easy pickings early on, with crayfish wandering about unable to find their way back to the ocean.

RNZ's Kate Newton reports how police, Department of Conservation and Red Cross people are discussing the crayfish conundrum at the emergency welfare centre at Ward Town Hall. One volunteer suggests that locals are putting them back in the water. 'Yeah, back from the sack that they've just put them into,' someone snorts. But Koko Lambert, who lives at Ward beach, says her husband is among those ushering the kōura back into the water. 'People were trying to get together to go to Cape Campbell to do the same ... If they're dead, they're no good to anybody.'

A pāua recovery group styles itself as the saviour of sealife in the face of uncaring officials, though scientists warn that prising the shellfish off rocks risks killing them, as they are haemophiliac. Mike Vincent and his team return thousands of pāua to the water before being stopped. 'We've got the support of the local iwi here, 150 per cent,' Mike says. 'This is wrong, what's going on, and I hope the right outcome comes of it, because if it doesn't, I'm not going to be coming here for probably 15 years of my life to get another pāua out of the water … We let it die, or we put it back in the water and give it a chance.

'At the end of the day, I'm here doing something because I see the disaster that's actually taking place,' Mike says. 'This man is sitting in an office, he's probably done a paper on it and he thinks that his words of wisdom are going to save this fishery in Kaikōura — it's not. Pāua don't live out of water.' Martine Martene says that the pāua are a precious taonga for the whole country. 'Everyone's involved, not just Māori,' says Martine. 'Everyone's involved, just to see the banding together between Māori and Pākehā brothers' — they add that Pasifika, American and French people have also been helping. 'Oh, this is huge,' says Mike. At one stage, the recoverists put out an estimate of having saved 50-plus tonnes of pāua.

Ministry for Primary Industries' Ben Dalton provides the counter-argument. 'I don't doubt for a minute, and having seen them in operation, that they're really well-intentioned; they have a real desire to try and do something about pāua. But what's not clear at the moment is whether their activities are assisting or harming the pāua stocks down here.' He says that the scientific advice from four sources is to leave the shellfish that are in the inter-tidal zone.

The story gets Twitter going, most of it unkind to MPI:

> what an awesome example of people! and what an
> awesome example of dumb bureaucrat decision
> making process
>
> — Samantha White, tweet

At South Bay, fisherman Paul Reinke is in a group gathered around fuelman Ken McKeown as he checks on the underground tank while the naval evacuation goes on. Paul's already caught a lot of his cray quota, so is in a better position than most. He's uncertain, though, what his next fishing trip will yield: 'We don't know till we get back out again and see whether the bottom's actually changed through our sounders and 3D imagery, see if the rocks have moved up or they're gone or whatever.' He has a jetboat, so might be able to use the marina as is. 'A few months ago we had quite a bit of survey work done for … when the tourist ships come in here, and they were having problems with their tenders coming in, et cetera, and so it was all surveyed. And I think next year we were going to have some work done with barges, et cetera, et cetera, so all that work's out the window and probably needs to be resurveyed and done again.'

He's still hanging on to a sliver of hope. 'Even though this is a phenomenon at the moment, this is only my opinion — we might not know much until a couple of days' time, until the moon subsides again … I hope so, but I don't think it is.'

The diver and the bubbles

'It was like a jacuzzi underwater.'
— Nigel Elson, to RNZ, Nov 25

Kayaker Matt Foy is the first to spot a mysterious line of bubbles breaking on the sea surface in Whaler Bay in the wake of the quake. He christens it 'Hope Springs'. It's an inspired choice. The UK's *Daily Mail*, never one to stint on hyperbole, waxes lyrical: 'Beauty among the devastation: Bizarre phenomenon sees plume of bubbles rise from the sea floor after deadly earthquake rocked New Zealand.' A scientist rather more prosaically explains that it's likely to be carbon dioxide rising from new cracks in the seabed, like fizz from a soft-drink, and is a fairly common phenomenon.

The town's divers aren't put off. Nigel Elson takes the first team in to have a look on November 25. They don't have to go far — just 1 to 3 metres down. 'It was like a jacuzzi underwater really, is probably the best way to describe it,' he tells RNZ's Jesse Mulligan. 'I was fully expecting to see a crack in the seabed, but there is no crack. It's literally just in a very clear line ... just coming through the rocks and sand ... There is certainly one big area where it's escaping rapidly, but the rest is just relatively small bubbles in a long line.

'I've managed to take a gas sample so if any of the professors are wanting to grab hold of that, just give me a call.' Jesse laughs: 'This is how scientific research takes place in New Zealand — someone grabs a gas sample, says if you want to get hold of it just give me a yell.' Dr Matthew Hughes of Canterbury University may do just that: he's dead keen on seeing locals and scientists teaming up to tackle some of the new geological and biological puzzles.

I cotton on that Nigel's going to check out the bubbles when I call Dive Kaikōura's Steve Blume to find out how he's doing. Not so good, it turns out. He's made a plea to Nathan Guy for urgent, compassionate consideration of his application to let divers swim with the seals. But there is a moratorium on this until 2025, because it's not known quite what effect the tourist attraction is having on the seals, and the Department of Conservation won't budge. Steve has only just bought his business off Nigel — and now has everything ahead of him and his five staff, even down to re-certifying all of the dive spots. According to the rules for adventure tourism, it's a new seabed so no one can be taken down until the dive spots have been given the all-clear. Steve is currently in Sydney where he operates a dive services business, and looking to fly over as soon as he can.

'Our compressor's been destroyed, our storage air banks have been destroyed, our high-pressure lines have been destroyed. Even our poor toilet has been destroyed,' he says. 'We've gotta do a fair bit of rebuilding just to get functioning. It's not like a shop where you've got T-shirts on the rack and you can open the doors and start trading. We have to have a very safe environment. We're working [with] up to 350 bar in pressure, and it has to be safe.'

He says he just wants to survive, but getting to the dive sites north or south is going to take a long time. 'So to be able to just dive in town, with those seals, is gonna be a life-ring, it really, really is.' However, the cumulative impact of renewed tourism is what worries Dr Sharon Goldstein, who's been researching seal breeding colonies in Kaikōura. 'What we know about the Kaikōura Peninsula from the uplift is it has had minimal uplift, but what now can happen, when the tourists do come back to Kaikōura, is that they now can walk out to where the breeding occurs.'

In early January 2017, I am back in Kaikōura on holiday and take the peninsula walk myself. A fair smattering of holiday-makers are about, and all of them are giving the seals a respectfully wide berth. Some of the rock pools are a little smelly, but smells and seals go hand-in-hand, and it remains a stunning walk.

———

The housebus and the convoy

'The advice at this stage is if you want to leave, is get down to the airport and charter an aeroplane …'
— RNZ reporter Conan Young, on RNZ, Nov 21

'I got the feeling that if there's major rain or shaking
there's more to move, more to come down.'
— a woman driving along the Inland Road to retrieve rental cars,
to RNZ, Nov 30

Two steps forward, one and a half back — that's how things
seem with the Inland Road. Early on, Transport Minister
Simon Bridges tells RNZ that it's looking like several days
before the Inland Road out can be opened, but not weeks. He
gets it right, sort of, if you count sporadic escorted convoys as
open. On Friday, November 25, Gary and Janine Smith join the
first civilian convoy out of Kaikōura on the repaired old state
highway via Waiau in their four-wheel-drive. Gary tells me that
it was so easy they could've taken their bus instead. 'Piece of
cake,' he says. 'Put it this way — we've got a 10.5-metre bus
motorhome and I wouldn't hesitate to take it through. I'd even
let my grandmother drive through in a shopping basket. We
didn't even think of putting this into four-wheel-drive, nowhere
near it.'

The road repairs are excellent, Gary says — just not the
communications. Janine tells me that if RNZ hadn't given them a
heads-up, they'd have missed the 1pm check-in on the Kaikōura
side. Someone who did miss it turned up the next day asking
whether they could drive out unescorted. A big no to that.

Fifty or so cars, four-wheel-drives, trucks and camper vans make
the first trip out; previously, only army convoys had been allowed

to do so. Yellow chits letting people stock up with 40 litres of fuel are being issued from the emergency centre in the town. 'It was very frustrating, because we were hearing stories [of] people coming out last week all saying that the road was good — and yet we were being told, when we rung up last night, that we needed a rugged four-wheel-drive. And I can tell you, you do not need a rugged four-wheel-drive to do that road,' Gary Smith says. 'The slips, though, are dangerous, and if there was a shake or heavy rain, I wouldn't like to be there.' He's just looking forward to hugging his daughter when he gets home.

That evening, Civil Defence says that the convoy has all gone incredibly smoothly and the road itself has held up well. But the very next day, this headline: 'Kaikōura convoy damaged "fragile" road'. Gary Smith had got it right when he surmised that it wouldn't take much for the Transport Agency to put a stop to people driving out. 'Another small earthquake or if the rain gets any worse, I think they would pull the pin sooner rather than later.' Another week on, and another week of roadworks and abseilers dislodging boulders from threatening slips, and the green light's given for more-regular civilian convoys. That's on the Wednesday. However, low cloud and drizzle puts paid to it that day. Overnight on Thursday there is steady rain, and that scotches any convoy for the entire weekend. It is an exercise in frustration for everyone.

Oaro and points south, you have not been forgotten

— Robert B Glennie, tweet, Nov 16

Regarding State Highway 1 north, there also is a fair amount of frustration. Gerry Brownlee gets into a spat with a Clarence farmer after the Acting Civil Defence Minister flies in in mid-December with just-appointed Prime Minister Bill English to talk about roadworks and announce that Cabinet's agreed to rebuild State Highway 1 and the railway line along the coast from Blenheim to Christchurch. The estimated cost is between $1.4 and $2 billion, and it's suggested there could be limited road access restored north of Kaikōura in a year, but this is ballpark to begin with — and looks much more so after I ask KiwiRail about it; they say that they haven't yet checked which out of four damaged tunnels they'll need to replace and which can just be repaired. In the chopper down, Bill English spots cars below and asks, 'Gerry, how are these locals travelling?' He's told there's been big progress in the eight days since his colleague was last in the air over the coast.

At Clarence, before heading to Kaikōura, both ministers are on the receiving end of a salvo from farmer John Murray in front of a gathering of locals. 'We had a meeting here three weeks ago and Gerry was here, and we left full of hope that something was going to happen,' John tells everyone. 'No one has attacked this northern end, the road's been open from Blenheim; no one's started tidying this road up at all, they've made patch-up repairs all the way through — and the roads from Ward and Waipapa Bay should have been upgraded and ready to go, so we could just go into the next stage.

'Nothing has been done except patch-up, and I reckon it's piss-poor, and if that's what our government feels about us, and how they deal with emergencies, then I'm afraid you have lost a lot of votes, and a lot of confidence in this area,' says John.

Gerry's not one to hold back, either: 'From our perspective, it's not easy. Sorry you're frustrated, but I'm pissed off that you took that attitude, quite frankly, and I've just sworn on TV.' John Murray retorts that 'I think you'll find everyone here thinks like I do', though one woman does speak up to disagree with his assertion that nothing's being done.

Brownlee shoots back: 'NZTA have not been sitting on their backside doing nothing, and quite frankly I resent your comments deeply ... The amount of work that's gone in to try and sort things out here is just extraordinary. I know you might be affected on your farm, but we are trying to get a solution to this problem that does not see us constantly coming back in what is very changing geology in years to come.'

He adds: 'We're also competing with people who are telling us what we can't do all the time, and there is many of them and there is thousands more than those who are telling us to get on with the job.' He has a point about the pressure: legislation is being hurried through to speed up the roadworks, allow slip debris to be shoved straight into the sea, and allow Kaikōura's rocky marina to be dredged — the ministers announced the provision of $5 million for that, too. University of Canterbury professor of marine science David Schiel has teams scouring the shore and reefs to build up a picture of what's changed. He warns that what is pushed into the ocean might end up near the shore and make the damage worse.

'In big loads, they smother things and they're [often] very hard to clear by natural processes, because they're what's called cohesive sediments — they sort of gloop together and sort of stay there,' he tells RNZ's Kate Gudsell. So even as tides and winds clear the reefs of the sediment that's already settled on them by natural processes, a whole lot more — and much more — might be deposited on them by human processes. 'The real question is: how limited is that inshore rocky reef along that area, and are we willing as a nation to sacrifice those reefs for a number of years in order to clear those roads?'

But as with the tourist evacuation, where cooperation eventually trumped frustration, time and effort — and some awfully big earthmoving equipment — begin to make a difference on the roads. On December 16, RNZ is able to report: 'The inland route to Kaikōura will open for unrestricted use next week for the first time since the November 14 earthquake. At the moment, route 70 can be used only by people who register the day before, and

carry safety gear. From Monday the road will reopen completely.'
Chris Robinson, who drives it on December 19, tells RNZ: 'The
road today is actually wicked — when the quake happened it was
pretty rough, but they've done a lot to it.'

The pie-seller and the truckies

'Normally there [are] 40 trucks a day. I think at the
moment it's up to 700, and next week would be the
biggest straight week of the year and it's likely to get
up over 1000 trucks.'

— Mainfreight boss Don Braid, to RNZ

People's disorientation has been paralleled by the dislocation
of the places where they live. St Arnaud on State Highway 63,
population a few hundred, finds itself suddenly on the route of
choice south from Picton to Christchurch now that the coastal
highway is blocked. Elaine Richards, who co-owns the town's
store and petrol station, sells a thousand pies in the week
following the quake — double the usual amount. Truck numbers
hit 400 a day, 10 times more than before. Truckies like pies. 'It
was overwhelming, actually, more than anything because some
of these trucks were huge,' she tells RNZ's Eva Corlett. 'We'd
never seen anything like that, and because we own a petrol
station where we are, a lot of the trucks … having to come the
long way had run out of petrol. That's where it came in for us.'

The business boom for St Arnaud, Murchison, Springs Junction and Culverden has its downside. On the last day of November, two trucks collide 9 kilometres north of Springs Junction, killing one person. Pictures show one truck on its side in a grassy ditch on a snaking piece of road. The route is closed for at least 12 hours. 'It's just not built to take it,' a Hurunui local tells me. I hear that Fulton Hogan has three crews running to a standstill out of Murchison just to keep State Highway 6, and 65 through the Lewis Pass, open. 'There's a lot of potholes blowing out and a lot of repairs going on. It's a work in progress,' says traffic controller Gary Tutty. And Christmas is coming. Normally, about 1200 cars and trucks (both ways) use the Lewis Pass each day, peaking at 3000 in summer. Add in the 2700 that use State Highway 1 north of Kaikōura on a regular day, and 5000 in summer, and that makes 8000 vehicles — including 500 trucks — through the Lewis Pass each day over the holidays.

A freight depot is set up at Spring Creek, just outside Blenheim. Other than that, the township has a superette on one corner, a service station on another, and a tavern on a third, recently bought by Mike and Hazel Pink. Although the chimney at the Junction Hotel has fallen down, they're busier than they ever imagined. 'We moved in on the fifteenth of October,' Mike tells RNZ's Tracy Neal. 'We had the ceiling come down in the restaurant, owing to a burst waste pipe upstairs, and numerous other things have gone wrong, but they've all been resolved and everything's hunky dory now.'

Ray Kendall from Auckland is now working at the new freight depot. 'We've been sent to help out, and I think we'll be here, back and forth, for about a year,' he says. Jason Tyrell lost his job towing trucks on and off the ferries in Picton after the quake. He's now driving freight seven-and-a-half hours to Christchurch. 'I had to find a job before Christmas, otherwise the kids won't have any presents.'

Further on, Wairau Valley Tavern owner David Jackson has a full pie-warmer even though it's gone 2pm. He's at the wrong part of the road and drivers aren't stopping. His old stagecoach tavern, built in 1880, has stood strong, however. 'Oh, we had a great ride on it — two minutes of rollercoaster heaven,' he tells Tracy Neal. Caridad Apas is parked beside the highway. She had been happy before, feeding the few passers-by from her mobile food business, Wheely Wild; now she's serving up to 150 cups of coffee a day, plus home-made wild venison pies. Before it wasn't really viable, but it was beautiful. Now it's both.

The stories I hear are enough to put me off our summer trip. The kids are going to a scout jamboree at Renwick Domain near Blenheim in late December; the leaders debate calling it off, but the fact that the 5000 children will be under canvas, not concrete, is enough to help swing the decision. That leaves me and my wife: we've rejigged our trip so that, rather than heading to Akaroa, we'll swing past Murchison and Mt Lyford and in to Kaikōura for a couple of days. There are myriad wild cards facing these sorts of trips: shakes, rain, crashes, jams, yes or no to a convoy (though on December 19 it's announced that the Inland Road is open to regular traffic again), and heavy traffic on once pretty sparsely-used roads. Thank God we're just on holiday and aren't making a living trucking freight or, worse still, relying on that freight to arrive to keep a business going.

The extent of the overall dislocation through the waist of southern New Zealand is difficult to gauge from either official announcements or local gossip, particularly as there is no publicly available overarching compilation of detailed engineering reports and contractors' assessments — not just of the scale of the job to clear the 28 moderate-to-major slips and repair or replace four road bridges between Cheviot and Ward, but also of the stability of the land any repaired road will run through and under. Which is to say nothing of the railway line. Which is also to say nothing of Wellington's CentrePort: the container park is badly damaged and will be out of action for months, reducing the potential for coastal shipping to take some of the load off the roads. The goalposts keep shifting as more information comes to hand, but 'huge and unprecedented' is the ballpark impact. Three weeks on, the government downplays a suggestion that it could be three years before State Highway 1 reopens in full. Yet it's also reported that the roadmaker Marlborough Roads has been told to prepare for three years of maintenance on State Highway 63.

'I went into the Bluebridge line [in Wellington]; there were possibly 10 or a dozen people waiting, including Bryce Mitchell from Ashburton. He had his race cars that he's had at Manfeild. He's expecting a long trip back to Ashburton, and then he's going to be back on the road 'cos he's a roading contractor; he's expecting he'll be sent to Blenheim to try and fix up the mess up there …'

— Phil Pennington, live-cross to RNZ *Morning Report*, Nov 14, 8.38am

Roading contractors will be flat-tack for months. Australian engineer Ian Waters writes to Civil Defence, suggesting that huge earthmoving equipment could be sent from across the Tasman. 'Driving home tonight past fleets of excavators and a lot of six-wheeled all-terrain dump trucks and 'dozers of any size up to D10s — all busy building a road for us to drive on in geologically stable NSW in a year or two's time — I'm thinking that right now your need is greater than ours,' Ian tells me. 'They could be on a ship in two days' time and on their way to you — together with plenty of operators, civil engineers, surveyors and whatever else you need. Concrete pumps, truckloads of high-quality Australian rebar and mesh, bitumen machines, screening plants, crushing plants, portable concrete batching plants, truckloads of cement and as many steel beams, columns and plate as you want … Our road can wait, mate.'

——

Roast lamb on the bricks

Just what we did too! (Chch 2011)

— Sarah Butterfield, tweet

The first RNZ team flies out of Kaikōura on Wednesday
afternoon, November 16, and we are replaced by the next crew:
Conan Young, Claire Eastham-Farrelly and Max Towle. They
arrive a lot better dressed than we were. A short time later, Conan
and video journalist Claire come across Gary Melville making the
best of it at his home with his wife, Gay. Conan tells their story:

*We initially stop to photograph a badly damaged home,
its brick cladding having fallen away completely on one
side and a blue tarpaulin the only thing protecting its
interior wall from the drizzle that's started falling. Gary
agrees to an interview and beckons me around the back to
where he's put some of his spare bricks to good use — as
a surround for a fire pit. No power or gas for the barbecue
means that this is his only means of preparing a cooked
meal, which tonight is slow-cooked lamb. 'Because
we're really low on gas — like an idiot I wasn't really
prepared, although we were prepared in a lot of ways, but
you couldn't find anything anyway, it was all buried and
trashed — so we had to find some [way] to cook so we've
organised this,' says Gary.*

*'We've always had those sort of Dutch oven things and
we had a lot of camping gear, so it was just really an*

opportunity to pull it all out and have the camping trip that we never had because we were always too busy. So we're kind of liking it really, we're not sad.'

Dinner tonight is a fore-quarter of lamb out of the freezer. 'The freezers aren't working, of course, so everything's going downhill, so we're, ah, living pretty high on the hog at the moment, eating as much as we can so we don't waste it. But we are starting to lose stuff, so we've dug a hole in the chook yard and [we're] burying it. And unfortunately the chooks have stopped laying, they're not happy.'

I ask if they can have a peek at how the lamb's doing. 'Okay, we'd better have a wee look; it's early days, I've just put it in there,' says Gary. 'I'm going to flash it up with herbs and stuff shortly, but it will be on there all day and by this evening it will be just fall-apart ... I don't want to say I'm really enjoying it, because our house has been trashed and we've lost so much of our little knick-knacks and treasures, it's real sad like that — but, you know, it's sort of exciting really, no work tomorrow.'

Gary and Gay have been in the house 30 years and in Kaikōura 'all our lives really'. His parents bought the place in the 1960s. 'Soon as I was old enough to leave school, though, post-Vietnam and all that, everyone wasn't interested in uni — just wanted to get out and get a bit of life before it all came crashing down with the Cold War

— so I went out flatting for a few years, and then when my parents died I bought it and I've been here ever since.'

Gary shows me around inside, where he and his wife have mostly managed to restore some order. A few corners haven't been got to yet; piles of books and broken glass point to the force of the earthquake. In the garage, bottles of home brew have smashed and heavy shelves have toppled over. Tools, carefully hung on a shadow board, have been put back in their places, waiting to be used to repair the damage we see around us. Miraculously, Gary's preserves have all remained upright, and the vegetable garden and fruit trees are still on track to produce a bumper harvest.

They're hoping to stay. 'Absolutely. Yeah no, we love it here. Kaikōura's such a great place, too, wonderful people. Pretty busy in the summer with tourists and everything, but you get your town back in the winter and it's just wonderful.'

News that supplies are running low at the town's only supermarket has some worried, but I get the feeling that Gary isn't among them. As he shows me around, I get a sense of the pride he has in his various endeavours, using skills that have obviously been passed on from his parents who had this place before him — the sort of self-reliance common back in the day. These skills come in to their own at a time like this, and allow people like Gary to seize back control of their lives at a time when others would feel overwhelmed.

———

Skaters

Step on a crack … you'll stack! Savage

— Sean Cupples, tweet, Nov 20, 10.12am

Photographer Tomoki Peters sees pictures of the damaged roads, and it reminds him of how skaters tried out Christchurch's damaged roads. He puts a call out online to any skater friends who want to head north to try it out. Troy Tapara and Billy Mclachlan go with him. Billy posts video of their rides showing him doing a frontside 50–50, skating down the highway towards a waist-high ledge formed where the entry to a bridge has cracked right the way across, and jumping off it onto the steel safety barrier before dropping back to the road.

Troy writes in *Manual Magazine*: 'After failing to reach the town of Oaro just south of Kaikōura on Saturday, a return visit was needed to session this earthquake-damaged bridge; when we drove up the following day, hype levels were at an all-time high. Both sides dropped around 1.2 metres, making it unusable for cars but perfect for Billy to pull out his old faithful, a 50–50. Billy warmed up, getting used to the rough state highway ground, then gave it a few pops, landing, then rolling away.'

On to it alright

— Quynn Stead-Hill, tweet, Nov 21

In another clip, they leap up and over the ledge; and in another, swerve up and over a big hump, taking out a full lane of the tarseal. Billy's board falls deep inside a crack and he has to reach in to get it. The pick of the clips is the three of them, one after the other, jumping a crack then down a drop in the road: 35,000 views and counting.

6

NOVEMBER: SECOND TRIP

'Tragedy quickly becomes drudgery, and drudgery is not news.'

— opinion piece in *The Guardian*, after the 2015 Nepal earthquake

'What are we hoping for? Things back to normal.'

— Geoff Pacey, to RNZ

Getting back in

'I can't wait, I'm so excited to see everyone again.'

— Savannah Manawatu, to RNZ's Conan Young

Wednesday, November 30, 11am

I am sitting in a café at Christchurch airport on my second large cup of Americano, at the start of my second trip into Kaikōura. It's drizzly upcountry, with low clouds. Sounds Air has already cancelled the 10am and the noon flights. Video journalist Claire Eastham-Farrelly is on her third cup. I haven't brought a change of trousers or a spare shirt, keeping things light so that Claire can get all 30 kilos of her camera gear on the small plane. Our last hope is the 2pm flight.

At the other end, in Kaikōura, the RNZ crew of Chris Bramwell and Kate Newton, who've been there since the previous Friday, are champing to get out. A booking muck-up means that Sounds Air can't take them, so their hopes rest on a charter flight. But when Sounds eventually cancels its 2pm, then RNZ pulls the plug on the charter, too. Too marginal.

'QUAKE LATEST: Controlled public convoys in and out of Kaikōura to begin tomorrow'

— RNZ, headline, Nov 29, 5.32pm

Chris and Kate suggest that they try to get in the convoy due to come out through the Inland Road at 2pm, the second — and last — one of the day. Yesterday, Civil Defence put out a detailed update, one that many people had been hoping for, saying that regular civilian convoys through the repaired road to Culverden would begin, two per day — until now, the only civilian convoy in or out has been the outbound trip on November 25. And indeed about 50 cars, utes and vans set out from the Mt Lyford end just after eight o'clock this morning. The first of them gets to the Kaikōura cordon at about 11am — a 3-hour journey along a 50-kilometre stretch of road. But it's a one-off. Later in the day, having retreated to RNZ's Christchurch office to wait for a flight on Thursday, we learn that the return convoy out of Kaikōura has been cancelled after a day of drizzle creates a high risk of rockfalls and landslides. Our colleagues are stuck, and we are stuck, and many, many others are also stuck. For many of them, the dislocation caused to their regular lives by the fragility of Kaikōura's lifeline is much more pronounced than it is for us.

Sixteen-year-old Savannah Manawatu, however, is happy. Evacuated by the air force on November 14, she now makes it back to Kaikōura in the early convoy. She tells RNZ's Conan Young that she's looking forward to seeing her parents. 'I can't wait, I'm so excited to see everyone again, it will be so good. I've missed them, of course, like I've been a bit nervous for them and scared in case another one hits.'

Roofing contractor Ray Fisher left Nelson at 2am to get to the in-bound convoy. But at the checkpoint he's told he can't take in his trailer loaded with construction materials. 'All the team above me have organised just to come in here, so I don't see why it's changed,' he tells RNZ. A debate ensues; eventually he is allowed through with the trailer, unimpressed at the mixed messages they're receiving from the authorities. By Friday — the first day of December and the first day of summer — heavy rain overnight and persistent drizzle throughout the day puts paid to all convoys, not just for Friday but for the entire weekend. The Transport Agency says that the wet weather has significantly increased the risk of travelling on a route that's already fragile.

While we wait on alternative arrangements to get in, I make a few calls and get hold of Dr Chris Henry. He's in Oaro, just south of Kaikōura, where he's flown in by chopper — a whiz-bang arrival to deliver bog-standard medical care. Chris is standing in the living room of local fire chief Vern McAllister, having a quick natter before he parks himself in Vern and his wife Sally's 6-metre-long caravan to begin the day's clinic. Twenty-one appointments are lined up already, and he has a few house visits after that. Not just to unsettled elderly folk, says Vern, who's 74. 'Some of them are struggling mentally — grown men crying. One bloke's lost his homestead, three generations he knows of have lived there.' Vern knows the people, knows what they need: a medical clinic in his caravan, the fire trucks parked up his driveway to make room in the brigade's garage for what Vern calls 'the country's only free supermarket — all the supplies are stacked up there and you just turn up and take what you need'.

> 'Somebody had a broken ankle — they'd walked
> around all week on it.'
>
> — Chris Henry, to RNZ

You can never have too much of this type of resilience, but staunchness can go too far. Chris is seeing his fair share of this. 'Up north at Clarence and Kēkerengū ... there's been a lot of land damage up there, so there's been some fairly stressed people and there's quite a few injuries that have been accrued, in mending the fencing and doing the work,' he tells me on the phone from Oaro. 'You don't know what you don't know, so that's why we're here really, 'cos I think people are so staunch ... At the end of last week we had one day where we had four broken limbs, all of which had been acquired in the earthquake a week before, and people had just carried on tidying up their property ... One guy had been fencing all week and thought, "Bugger, my hand's still really sore," and I said, "Well, that's 'cos it's broken."' Chris chuckles.

'Somebody had a broken ankle — they'd walked around all week on it. [There was] an ankle, a wrist, a finger ... They all just hadn't complained; said, "Oh, you're busy up there, didn't want to bother you with it," hoped it would get better and just kind of stomped around for a week.' Chris tacks on the advice that it's better to seek medical help quickly, before an injury gets worse. Yet it's clear he gets how people feel. How could he not, living as he does up the back of beyond in the Clarence, where the only bridge is now out? 'These are pretty uncomplaining people who just get on with it,' he says.

———

Lake Rebekah or Lake Quake

'… who doesn't like lakes?'

— Rebekah Kelly, to RNZ, Dec 2

Thursday, December 1, 10am

We fly to Kaikōura with Hugh Robinson, who runs two Cessnas at Air Canterbury when he's not farming. We fly over his land at Hurunui, and shortly afterwards he sweeps to the left to show us landslide damage he's never seen the like of before. 'Look at that,' says Hugh. A great cheese-block of scrubby farmland — Hugh reckons it is 500 metres square and the same high — has shifted sideways by 600 metres, creating new gullies, dams and slopes. A pine plantation to the right looks as if a giant hand has patted the trees down like dog fur; some lean this way, others that. A minute further on we get to the site of Hugh's favourite story. A wee lake appears — a kilometre or so long, and rising; it's brand-new, he tells us, and the farmer has called it after herself.

I phone this through to RNZ, and producers get hold of Rebekah Kelly. She gives *Morning Report* four photos shot between November 16 and 28, showing the lake filling up behind a landslide dam. 'The dam is so big that I can be either happy or unhappy if I choose,' she says. 'But you've got to find some excitement in these things, and for my children — we home-school them here, and so this place is as much our playground as it is our place of business — and who doesn't like lakes?'

This fifth-generation farming family got an early clue as to what was happening on their Woodchester farm as they stood with their kids in the big paddock they had fled to during the quake. 'Once the rocking stopped, we heard this other noise,' says Rebekah. 'And my husband said, "Well, what do you think that is?" and I thought, "Well, the only time I've ever heard that noise was a river being quite big and doing big-river things," so I just said, "Oh, it's just probably the river."'

On a drive around there, Dave Kelly finds out just what the noise was. 'So he came back in the next day and said, "You'll just never believe what has happened."' It turns out that a whole hillside, and the big terrace in front of it, has slid away. 'I think the scientists said it's 13 million tonnes of dirt in it, and as perspective I think the Manawatu Gorge slip that took months and months to clear was 200,000 tonnes, so it's just massive,' says Rebekah. She rushes to Facebook to announce that she's naming the new landmark after herself — Lake Rebekah — before the children can christen it Lake Quake.

'It's nothing we ever could have conceived would happen,' she says, reaching for the upside of the event. 'Sheep and beef farming being what it is, you look for other income streams; and tourism was something that we had thought about, but never conceived that we'd wake up in the morning to a lakefront property.'

———

Joe makes a sale

> 'The guys flew into Kaikōura to check out our facility and do [their] bit to help the locals who were needing fuel. They reckoned the reception they received was that fantastic they decided to stay — well, that and they couldn't get a helicopter out!! To the people of Kaikōura you make us proud to be [K]iwis.'
>
> — McKeown Petroleum on Facebook, Nov 18, 2.14pm

Thursday, December 1, 1pm

The town is definitely humming compared with two weeks before, when I was last here. We see three, maybe four cars on the highway during the 5-kilometre drive in from the airport. The slump-slalom course up the hill has been filled in and packed with gravel, and it's a two-way road now. The vehicles corralled around the hospital are mostly gone. The marae is quiet: relief operations have moved to the primary school beside the rugby ground, though those are also winding down. The scores of rental cars and camper vans that filled up the school playing field when the tourists were flown out are mostly gone, too, and the children are back in class, mostly (perhaps a fifth have not made it back to town yet). I hear that up at Kēkerengū the school bus started back up again yesterday, carrying children up to Ward School. The shops down below on West End are open, mostly. It's bright and sunny again. It feels hopeful. Mostly.

Joe van Rooyen meets us outside the rental property he's just sold along Beach Road, up by the New World and the Lobster Inn. His white Mercedes SUV is parked up; the real estate business must have been doing okay. Joe's been selling homes and businesses around the district for 25 years; he was the original one-man-band when he started, but three or four other agents have set up since. Joe has a lot of experience, but has no precedent for what has happened here, or what to do about his daughter's place. Although intact on its concrete slab foundation, it has tilted so much that a marble will run happily downhill along the floor. It'll be an EQC and insurance matter, says Joe. What's most crucial, he reckons, is for geotechnical engineers to suss out the land itself in the hardest-hit, low-lying land to the north of town, on the west side of Beach Road alongside a stream there and around Mill and Mount Fyffe roads, to determine whether anyone should be building there in future. One prospect, he says, is to shift all new development up to the hill, up on the rock.

One of the properties on the vulnerable side of Beach Road is the Lobster Inn. Trish Mulvaney lives out the back in a community of a dozen permanent caravans with add-on rooms, a project the inn's owner, Neil, has been working on for eight years. Trish's van jumped off its supports and the front room pulled away. 'And I'm one of the lucky ones, 'cos behind me people lost their caravans, camper vans, all just slipped away ... Because we have the creek behind us, everything just sort of gave way and went down into the creek. We have big gaps in the pavement and driveway, you know, 6 or 7 feet, you couldn't even see the bottom — they're just massive.' Neil's been pulling the vans and cars out using a Hiab loader crane, she says. The quake hasn't put her off living there, though. 'My neighbours next door, they left, they were too terrified to stay ... But everyone just comes together down there — even the two [people] who were temporary, they still want to stay and be part of our little commune down there ... It's actually brought us together a lot more, too. And a caravan moves with the motion, so it's the best place to be.'

This place is home for her and her 56-year-old galah, Joey, who once belonged to her father. The night of the quake, the bird was out of his cage in the van as usual. 'He started making a noise and next thing everything shook, and I fell out of bed and all hell broke loose, yeah. Took off to the top of the hill.' Joey stayed behind. 'When I actually got home, the funny part of the story is, he was still walking around the back yard,' says Trish. 'So he stayed at home and after about an hour I thought, "Oh no, my gosh, Joey," but I was too scared to go back home and see — and he was still there early in the morning, walking around the yard, having a look in my fish pond. He come runnin'. He knows the sound of my voice and the car.' The galah lost a bit of weight, but has fattened up again; he's shaken his feathers and got on with it, like Trish.

On the seaward side of Beach Road, Joe van Rooyen takes us through the three-bedroom house he's sold. Claire gets footage of the butterscotch interior décor that's certainly seen better days; the picture window that's cracked; the hot-water cylinder that burst in the quake, flooding the kitchen. The house sold for $280,000 — about the same price as it would have fetched pre-quake, Joe says.

He's sensing signs of a new source of demand, after taking calls from several out-of-town investors. 'Had a good conversation with one of them — he said [he'd] bought several rental investment properties in Christchurch and done very well out of it. And he wanted to be in quick here and do the same.' Rentals have already been in tight supply in Kaikōura, and demand can only go up as more people's homes are declared unsafe or they make their own choice not to go back.

Joe had another 10 deals on the go when everything went topsy-turvy; three have gone through, but seven now need more work doing on them, such as a geotechnical report for a large block of farmland north of town. The Australian buyers of a café in town are now renegotiating, as the income forecasts have changed. Joe's just got an engineer's sign-off for one property that will keep a big commercial deal on track — he won't say much about that one. Two months previously, he negotiated the sale of the landmark Adelphi Hotel, which now stands out for another reason — it has the most security fencing and warning tape surrounding it of any property on the shopping strip. The hotel had already needed to be quake-strengthened; now the damage to its floors may just mean its demolition and possible replacement.

Joe has been chairing the trust that got the new hospital built — and not on the site of the town's tip, where there was early official pressure to put it. Up by the park, it proved to be the community's single most important resource and refuge in this disaster. He's used to getting things done. 'We'll be okay,' he says.

———

The ex-stripclub owner and the ruined dream

> 'I reckon it will be another five years before we get anybody seriously looking.'
> — Colin Hensley, to RNZ, Nov 30

Thursday, December 1, 3pm

Twenty kilometres to the south, in the seaside settlement of Oaro, Colin Hensley is not feeling optimistic. I call him on the phone when Claire spots his house advert on TradeMe. Colin listed the solid, two-bedroom wooden home as a private sale on November 4; it is undamaged. 'We had one guy was very, very keen, was going to come up on the Thursday — we had the bloody earthquake on the Monday,' says Colin, 69, who'd run a stripclub in Nelson before choosing the quiet life on the coast with his partner, Wendy Brewerton. 'He rung up ... said, "Are you all right?" and we said, "Yes," but there was no mention of the house or looking at the house.'

Even if it sold right now, he reckons the house's value might have fallen from $170,000 to $150,000 or lower, but he doubts it will move. 'I reckon it will be another five years before we get anybody seriously looking.' The hardest thing is that Wendy desperately wanted to go to Richmond to look after her four grandchildren for her daughter, who's not well. They had planned to buy and live in a big caravan so they could go touring occasionally. These plans are now on hold.

Colin and Wendy's neighbour, 74-year-old fire chief Vern McAllister, is cheerfully unperturbed. He and wife, Sally, had been looking to sell so that they can take off touring in their 6-metre caravan, to go trout-fishing. 'We are selling because we want to have a look around the South Island and maybe in the winter go north, but we absolutely love it here so we are under no pressure to sell — we are very happy to stay here another year if it takes that long to settle down.' Vern, who must be at the window, tells me he can see seven fallow deer grazing on the slope above the house. 'If you wanted to, you could shoot them

— we have a cup of tea and admire them. It's a gorgeous spot … my biggest problem is the bellbird, and he doesn't recognise daylight saving, so 5.30 every morning he goes off outside my window.' They won't list the property now. And what about a drop in its value? 'Well, I really can't say.'

Lynne Hastie lives in Mount Fyffe Road, in the hard-hit, low-lying land a couple of paddocks down from Mark Solomon's ruined home, and a few hundred metres along from the Old Convent, a two-storey wooden home all taped up and with ugly cracks in the concrete chimney above the tin roof. We're driving by, and stop at a 'For Sale' sign — Lynne hasn't got round to taking it down yet. The Hasties have been driven out of their 1992 house and into their 1930s stucco rental. 'We had our front property here on the market and we live in our back property, which was severely damaged by the earthquake,' she tells me. 'So we have had to move out of our back property back into our front one, until we get our back property assessed as to whether it's got to come down or not.'

Local book-keeper John McDonald has taken up the task of convening the professional services businesses group, which includes real estate, within the wider Kaikōura recovery group. 'Basically, the merry-go-round has stopped. And everybody's got off,' he says. 'And now we have to work out how to start the merry-go-round again and get on with business.'

Cancellations all round

'Tough times have hit again and our hotel … has been red stickered and cordoned off. Struggles are daily. If you feel compelled please visit'
— Michelle Beri, of Waiau Lodge Hotel, on Facebook

'It's just soul-destroying.'
— Eve Parkin of Peketa Beach Holiday Park, to RNZ, Nov 17

On this second trip, I call around some tourism operators to see what is happening. Holidaymakers are cancelling bookings in Kaikōura at an alarming rate, in some cases for months ahead. By late November, the five-star Fairways apartments on Ocean Ridge, just south of town, has lost $60,000 of forward bookings. The Gateway Motor Lodge scrubs half its bookings; so, too, the rustic Goose Bay motor camp and the $200 per person per night luxury Camp Kēkerengū that offers glamping 60 kilometres to the north.

In response, one top-end operator offers big flight subsidies. The up-to-$1000-a-night Hapuku Lodge and Tree Houses offers a sweetener of $250 a night off the room rate to subsidise the chopper or fixed-wing flight in. General manager Chris Sturgeon tells me it's vital to keep his 19 staff on until things pick up, and the government subsidy is crucial for that. 'If we lost our chefs we'd be in dire straits.' He has the staff doing all the winter jobs, cleaning and staining and painting. Gerald Noble's doing the same at the Top 10 Holiday Park in town — 'We'll have the cleanest camp in New Zealand with no tourists in it,' he jokes.

Chris Sturgeon's clientele may have deeper pockets than most, but their qualms are similar. 'We would have certainly lost a good 50 per cent of our bookings in December, but we are only down just on 19 per cent of our bookings for January, and we put a lot of that down to the subsidy … and at the moment we're not seeing a heck of a lot out of February,' Chris tells me. 'But on the positive side … we've seen in the vicinity of a good dozen, maybe 20, requests for accommodation in December and January of people wanting to come … recognising that Kaikōura needs support and they've always wanted to visit us, so they're coming out of Nelson, coming out of Christchurch.'

Pip Todhunter and husband, Simon, who run Camp Kēkerengū on their beef and sheep farm above State Highway 1, are experiencing the same thing. They've just booked in some Filipino tourists prepared to drive the eight hours around from Christchurch via Blenheim to get to the three-tent glamping site with its view out over the Pacific Ocean. 'A lot of the people who have booked and now can't get here, have kept their money with the company and they're gonna rebook for next year, which is a positive sign for us … Yes, it is good. We've had a huge number of people wanting to come here, so if they really want to get here, they still will.'

The Todhunters sank $100,000 into setting up the glamping in the summer of 2015, and were going gangbusters. 'In hindsight, if we had known the road was going to be closed, we wouldn't do it,' says Pip. 'We were fully booked pretty much every night from a couple of weeks ago to the middle of January, but now we have had a huge amount of cancellations due to the road.'

Liz Henderson takes bookings for Camp Kēkerengū. 'Any domestic bookings that were Christchurch-based have cancelled, mainly due to just being traumatised by the quakes — being scared or their children being scared, or just feeling like they just don't want to leave home right now,' Liz says. The backpacker end of the market doesn't get the buffer provided by tourists with deep pockets: Bad Jelly backpackers' Mike Toni loses all the bookings he had lined up in December. Dave Stanford cancels everything at his two hostels until the end of January.

The operators band together to plan a strategy, not only for luring tourists back but also for getting the supplies they need — something that's proving difficult. Kathy Christian gets hold of just one delivery of clean linen in the fortnight after the quake: the service she uses, Bays Laundry in Motueka, delivers the sheets by fishing boat, as air delivery would simply cost too much. Liz and John Mahony have a bigger problem: while they're allowed back to their home after 10 or so days of being evacuated because of the Ote Makura landslide dam, their Goose Bay motor camp remains closed as it's on lower ground. 'We've even got people cancelling in January,' Liz says, reckoning she's fielded 20 such emails in the past day or two. She voices a common call — of desperation, of needing to get a clearer steer from the authorities on just when State Highway 1 to Christchurch might reopen. A week or so later, the word goes out that there should be single-lane access before Christmas; perhaps even regular access.

At the Waiau Lodge Hotel, a temporary bar is set up after the grand old two-storey building itself is red-stickered. A big fireplace has showered hefty bricks all around the existing bar. Co-owner Michelle Beri lost her house in the Christchurch quake. She gets a nasty surprise this time round from her insurance company. 'We were fully covered on the material, but not natural disaster cover,' she tells John Key in early December when he tours the district. It makes a big difference, she says. 'So now we've only got the building covered — all our plant, stock is all gone, business interruption, we get nothing. So currently we're sleeping in the car park, I'm in a caravan that's borrowed, and Lindsay's in the shed.'

Landslides and dams

'These dams are not all full, so we do have a little bit of time.'

— Sally Dellow, at a Civil Defence briefing, Dec 1

Thursday, December 1, 7pm

On our way to Max Scattergood's to find out where his brewery is at, Claire and I stop by the district council office on the off-chance they've an update worth hearing. They certainly do. The main news, initially at least, is that 12 out of 29 evacuated households are being allowed back into Goose Bay. A GNS team has been using laser topography equipment and a drone to build up a 3D model of the landslide dam on the Ote Makura Stream flowing into the bay, and they're now confident that houses in the higher parts of the settlement will be okay if the dam breaks. The other 17 households aren't happy, but have accepted the situation.

As GNS engineering geologist Sally Dellow is wrapping up a media briefing that has shrunk to just three news teams, I ask about the other landslip dams in the district. It turns out that they have just completed a 10-day aerial survey that's found 150 such dams, 11 of which need a close eye kept on them. Some of these are close to breaking, and they are doing two or three flyovers a week, along with a lot of detailed engineering to assess the risks. GNS's early modelling suggests that 8 of the 11 dams won't cause downstream flooding if they break; for the other three, including the Ote Makura Stream dam, more calculations are being done. Linton Creek has a high chance of failing, and poses a risk — albeit a low one — to an Inland Road bridge with particularly low clearance and to Lynton Downs School in the flood plain. The tiny school has been warned and has an evacuation plan.

'Our initial modelling, based on estimates, has shown that the school is not going to be inundated if that [dam] breaks — but again, we have got to go and measure it and redo it, make sure we get down to the right answer,' says Sally Dellow. 'The dams are up in the high country and there's a wide flood plain before you get to the Inland Road, so our determination is that the water, by the time it gets to the bridges, is going to go under the bridges and not affect the Inland Road.'

The rock dams formed from greywacke, such as those above the road on the Conway and Towy rivers, are draining better than the others. The Leader River has two very large landslides on it, one of which has created Lake Rebekah.

'We've developed a priority list, kind of from our collective experience and knowing what's the risk downstream. These dams are not all full, so we do have a little bit of time,' says Sally Dellow.

We're able to package this information up for *Morning Report* the next day, and do a live-cross to the programme from the Hapuku River, 10 minutes north of town.

———

Friday, December 2, 7am

It begins raining late on Thursday, and at 6am on Friday it is still persisting down. We have RNZ rainjackets, but I'm aware that my decision to not bring a spare pair of trousers might be coming back to bite me. Claire drives us north in a hired four-wheel-drive on a deserted State Highway 1. We turn off down a gravel track leading to the Hapuku's riverbed from where I do a live-cross to Kim Hill on *Morning Report*:

> *Kim Hill:* 'Phil Pennington is at the Hapuku River downstream from one of the biggest landslides. Hi Phil.'
>
> *Phil Pennington:* 'The rain is falling very heavily, it has since about 10 o'clock last night; we're getting fairly wet here in the Hapuku River valley, just standing in front of the State Highway 1 bridge … In front of me two rivers [are] running together, one is running quite greenish, the other one quite brown, and I can only surmise that that perhaps is running under that dam that's up in the foothills, and that is a 150-metre-high slip that has got water in behind it …
>
> 'There is a flyover [by the scientists] today, the last flyover was on Monday … Actually there was meant to be a flyover today, I must say with this weather and the low cloud I guess they won't be having one, and I don't know how concerned they would be about this amount of water falling into those dams behind those landslides.'
>
> — RNZ *Morning Report*, Dec 2, 7.15am

Kim then asks me what we are doing in the riverbed. It's a good question. 'We came down here for atmosphere, Kim,' I reply. 'I am beginning to wonder [about] that myself ... We might retreat.'

Civil Defence is advising people to stay out of the river valleys. Drenched at Hapuku, Claire and I are happy to comply.

———

Between the slips

> '... the steel railing, designed to prevent cars from plunging into the sea, spirals out into thin air over the rocks and waves beneath us. This does not feel safer than the tunnel.'
> — Conan Young, RNZ reporter, Dec 7

RNZ video journalist Bex goes on three forays to Kaikōura. On the third, on December 7, she's intent on pushing north beyond the town and beyond Hapuku, where a big slip blocks the way. She and RNZ colleagues Conan Young and Patrick O'Meara set out early, and when they get to the 'Road closed' sign, keep going another 1 or 2 kilometres, as the locals are doing. They park up rather than follow the track others have made with their four-wheel-drives — down onto the beach and around the foot of the first mega-slip that's covering the highway. Armed only with the lights of their cellphones, they head into tunnels. At one point they have to crab across the face of a slip. 'That was hairy as hell,' Bex says. 'Boulders the size of cars. I couldn't help but think, "I'm only 60 kilos, but if I pick the wrong boulder and it collapses more boulders … And what if there's another aftershock?"'

Conan Young tells his story:

We leave the car just past the 'Road closed' sign, having come to the first slip barring our way. A temporary road veers around the pile of rocks, a bumpy detour we decide not to risk in the hire car. It doesn't take long before we come to the first truly big landslide — extending hundreds of metres and all the more pronounced due to the trees along its edge that haven't yet given way.

My stomach churns each time I look up the hill, and the ground beneath my feet starts to feel less stable than ever. Thoughts quickly turn to where the quickest means of escape is, in case there's another shake and the rocks start to move again. We're not alone, and are passed by trucks heading slowly along the makeshift road around the slips and up Blue Duck Valley, where work repairing an inland road continues.

Then we see the train, famously trapped between the landslides when the earthquake struck; now the target of looters. To reach it we have to decide whether to brave the train tunnel ahead of us or cross the slip over the mangled road above. We figure the tunnel's the safest option in case there's another shake, guessing that it will at least provide shelter from any falling debris, and edge forward.

An even worse landslide sends us into the next tunnel where the locomotive has been parked — we assume as protection from falling rocks. Just as we enter, we look back and see a policeman where we've just come from, and return to check that we're not doing anything illegal. He's here to relieve some tired locals, and while he doesn't recommend that we proceed any further, there's nothing he can do to stop us. After agreeing to take photos of any looters we come across, we continue — over the slip having been told that the tunnels are too dangerous.

Huge boulders force us to walk along the busted edge of the road where the steel railing, designed to prevent cars from plunging into the sea, spirals out into thin air over the rocks and waves beneath us. This does not feel safer than the tunnel. The 40-odd train carriages just beyond the second tunnel seem to go on forever.

Large boxes lie strewn on the ground nearby, where looters have picked through them for anything valuable and easy to carry out. There are all manner of things: plastic drink bottles, stationery, an engine; goods bound for destinations south of here that will now be sorted out by the insurance companies.

The road ahead is quiet apart from bird-song, there's very little wind and it's overcast, adding to the sense of suspended animation. Out to sea, we see a white line around the base of the rocks, evidence of the uplift. We later hear reports of strange sounds coming from under the sea straight after the earthquake. The pāua and crayfish that people here rely on for their incomes are left stranded in the open air and are slowly dying. Seals venture close to the road, enjoying not having to share it with traffic.

I've travelled along this stretch of State Highway 1 too many times to remember, and was always struck by its beauty: the ragged rocks, the native bush coming right down to the road, the back-drop of the mountains that rise steeply behind it all. Without the constant rush of traffic moving north and south, the sound of the sea and the birds becomes sharper, adding to the majesty of the place. But there's a sense of unease as well, a feeling things aren't as they should be.

Up ahead we see a large rock sitting in the middle of a stretch of otherwise undamaged road. There's no obvious sign of where it might have come from — it looks as if it's been just chucked there. A little further on, we come to the tiny settlement of Rakautara, a dozen houses and eight inhabitants on a narrow strip of land. Smoke's rising behind one property, and out the back we find Tahua Solomon cooking something up for his dogs. He and

Ngaio Te Ua invite us in for a cup of tea and some broken biscuits — 'earthquake biscuits', they call them.

On the night of the quake, fearing a tsunami, they join a convoy of locals and tourists desperate to escape to higher ground further down the road at Mangamaunu. But they are cut off. 'As you can see it's just total devastation, destruction — the whole hill has fallen on top of the tunnels, unbelievable,' says Ngaio. With escape southwards out of the question, Tahua checks on the highway heading north, but makes it only a few kilometres to Ohau Point. 'From there, you couldn't distinguish a road. It's just like the side of a mountain, and part of the side of the mountain is the train tracks that have come 20 metres from their bed and it's basically right across the road and in the ocean, so yeah — we knew we were stuck,' Ngaio says.

They retreat to their settlement. The aftershocks play havoc on the nerves, though their most immediate concern in those first few days is water. The pipes bringing it to them from a spring high up on the hill behind have burst. All they have is what's still in their tanks and any rainwater from their roofs — if it rains. The tanks run dry; fixing the pipes becomes the only option. Tahua's not looking forward to it — it means clambering up a steep hill among the loose boulders and scree slopes. 'It was scary getting up there. I don't know whether my mates were scared, but I was certainly quite windy about it,' he says.

The laborious task of reconnecting the pipes goes smoothly, until — with less than 100 metres left to fix — their way is blocked by a landslide. It's a small slip, but is almost vertical and falls at least another 100 metres to the ground. Anybody attempting to cross it is clearly going to be taking their life in their hands. A local self-confessed hermit, known only as Pete, rises to the occasion. 'He's a tiny wee waif and moves around really quickly,' says Tahua. 'We didn't want him to do it, but he insisted and he got the pipe across.'

It's a week before any help comes their way, though they have cellphone coverage and ring through to town. The first visit is from a chopper pilot who delivers food from the Kaikōura marae, the next from a farmer who lands his plane on the road. 'Next minute this guy comes in his little fixed-wing top-dressing plane and lands here on what we now call our airstrip, and he brought all of these supplies from these amazing people in Christchurch,' says Ngaio.

When we reach Tahua and Ngaio, it's just over three weeks since they were stranded on a virtual island: sea in front of them, mountains behind them, and the only road in or out blocked in both directions. The power has only recently been restored, but — like Gary Melville back in town — this couple knows how to live off the grid. They cook meat from a well-stocked freezer on a gas barbeque and an open fire, and a battery-powered radio has kept them in touch with news from outside.

Ngaio works for Whale Watch, and Tahua is a trustee for a local iwi. They've rented their small wooden cottage here for over a decade and want to stay, though the risk of boulders crashing down means that for now they need to sleep in a neighbouring building owned by their landlord. They can already see potential for Rakautara as a place for the road crews to stay. 'We have about two-and-a-half kilometres of road that we can race up and down, so the diesel four-wheel-drive — that's beginning to choke, because you never get it out of third gear,' he says with a chuckle.

I ask him whether Rakautara is considering declaring independence from the rest of the country. 'I think a lot of the people that live here have already declared that years ago [but] not us. I like being on the road to everywhere and having the ability to just move in any direction really, but that's stopped.'

'You could get from North Auckland to Invercargill on this road out in front of us,' adds Ngaio. She pauses, 'Yeah, it's a bit blocked at the moment.'

Conan, Bex and Patrick retrace their steps along the ribbon of ruptured foreshore, back to their four-wheel-drive, though this time they choose to go through the tunnel rather than across the slip. The locals tell them that's safer, and — once they get to the narrow squeeze between the abandoned train cab and the tunnel wall — to stick to the left since the cab is leaning towards the right-hand side.

To the south of town, the roadworks include abseilers prising boulders off slip faces using crowbars and inflatable bags. Alex Wilmshurst of Abseil Access smiles somewhat boyishly about this. 'Some of the rocks we were moving yesterday were up to 10 cubic metres — so some of them look quite small from below, but when you get up there, it's all quite fractured rock that we are removing. It's quite satisfying seeing them roll down the hill — we do have a little fun, but we're there to do a job as well.'

Choppers are using monsoon buckets dipped in the sea to sluice loose rock off the slip at Ohau Point, one of those that's cutting off Rakautara. The work's put on hold when the Ngāti Kuri hapū calls for checks to ensure that wāhi tapu urupā, sacred burial grounds, aren't being damaged. Ngaio Te Ua says that everybody wants the work done, but not at the expense of precious sites. 'I fully support Ngāti Kuri going in there with their teams to see whether this is being done. Whether they find any artefacts or urupā or remains, I think that the local iwi should be there.'

———

The great grandma and her 'little man'

'There's a whole new normal coming over the town as the reality of what's happened is setting in.'

— Lorraine Diver, to RNZ, Dec 2

Friday, December 2, 9am

Trish Mulvaney is sorting through donated clothes on the front bench of the jam-packed recycling-centre shop alongside the town's rubbish tip on Kaikōura Peninsula when I come in, needing a pair of dry trousers after the Hapuku River foray. For a dollar I get two pairs, a T-shirt and a sweatshirt. 'We were really, really flat-tack,' says Trish of the immediate post-quake period. 'Very inundated — run out of coat-hangers, mainly clothes, everybody seems to be re-doing their wardrobes ... seems to be a good excuse for everyone to be spring-cleaning.' They always had a bin for old crockery alongside the broken glass bin — 'it's just got a lot more in it now'. Little buckets of Christmas baubles, sorted by colour — mostly purple and red — sit on a table. A bloke goes out with an armful of clothes. Quite some time later he's back, to pay. Above Trish's head hang a dusty aeroplane and a helicopter made out of soft-drink cans. 'We call it Mitre 11,' she says. 'I've volunteered here for two years, which I love totally.'

It was big job cleaning it up on November 14. 'Everything was off the shelves, glass was all broken, china — so to get away from the quake I actually worked six days a week, as a lot of other people did ... At that time I was sleeping in my car. And this was the centre for everybody, you know; camper vans all use the facilities up here, yeah.'

Trish introduces me to Lorraine Diver, who's flicking through a clothes rack. 'We have been busy, yeah, yeah, but there's a whole new normal coming over the town as the reality of what's happened is setting in,' says Lorraine. 'Yep, so the town's starting to quieten down a wee bit as they're starting to absorb exactly what the reality is for the next few months.'

And what does that look like? 'The new reality is, for me, I've been here 36 years, and it's almost like we've gone back to 1980 again — the town has just gone quiet, very, very quiet. As much as I'm enjoying the quietness, you know, economically it's just not good for our town, so the sooner they get those roads open and that marina up and running, the better it's going to be for our town.

'We were a lovely little sleepy seaside town here in 1980, then thanks to government policies and restructuring we lost 52 families out of our community in the early 1980s — the railway, Ministry of Works, fisheries — and then thanks to the foresight of some local families, Whale Watch was born and the town has never looked back; it's been amazing, an amazing ride for the community … Whale Watch has been the best thing that ever happened to this community, it really has.

'What now? Well, I hope everyone will get their thinking caps on, because we're very good at doing that, and thinking outside the square and coming up with some new short-term initiatives that are gonna get this town through, yep.' Any good ideas out there? I ask Lorraine. 'I have heard some ideas but not to be made public at the moment,' she says. 'And those ideas have got to come from the people who've made those ideas.'

Trish Mulvaney whispers an aside to me that she won't mind if Kaikōura goes back to what it was like three decades ago. 'The old Kaikōura was nice, laid back … All the business people won't like that, but yeah it was a nice place. It still is, but it's very business[-like], whereas I just like beach walking and doing those things.' She is not alone: bach owner Keith Beardsley tells RNZ that tourism has not been an unalloyed good, noting how it has changed the village atmosphere in South Bay. Buses go backwards and forwards, ferrying people to different attractions. 'It resembles more of a pre-match at a rugby game,' Keith says.

For Trish Mulvaney, a few tourists or many — she won't really mind as long as she can still have her biannual family reunions here. She's had to cancel the Christmas 2016 one. It's too far, and things are too uncertain, for her son, Carl, and his Brazilian family who live in Brisbane to come. Right now they're in Brazil with her parents. Trish's caravan out the back of the Lobster Inn is back on its piles, but stability is at a premium right now. ''Cos there's no guarantee he'll get through, and it's so expensive to fly within the islands. Which is a shame, 'cos every two years my family all get together, all my children, grandchildren, great-grandchildren, that's our big family get-together … that's our time.' It was planned for Christchurch on Christmas Day, with everyone then chilling out at Kaikōura for five days.

'So that's gonna be a wee bit sad. But on the other hand, every second year, me and some of the oldies here get together and have our Christmas, so we're just going to do the oldies' thing again, and put our hats on and [have] our wine, down on the beach … We'll go down to Hapuku and sit on the beach in our hats and our wines, or in my case my bourbon. So that's all good, too, you know. And we'll speak to family, it just means the family's not going to be together this year.'

This family is now linked together in another way: by earthquakes. 'My little man, he was the last baby born in Christchurch before the earthquake, so his name is Leo Quake Jones,' says Trish. 'My little great-grandson … So he's been in the newspapers and all over the place … he's my little man.' She talked to Leo on the phone after November 14, and the six-year-old was worried and wanted her to come to stay with them. As she recounts this, Trish tears up for the first time. She takes a deep breath. 'But I couldn't. I just couldn't, I needed to be here, helping, so I told him about the helicopters coming and landing in the park, to distract him, you know.'

It is raining steadily as Claire and I leave the recycling centre.

———

The rubbishman's plea

'We saw there were a lot of mistakes made when they
threw a lot of money at it in Christchurch with rebuilds,
so let's just hope it doesn't happen here — mistakes.'
— Geoff Pacey, to RNZ, Nov 15

Remaking the town and district is taking place by way of negotiation and debate, push and shove — including with robust Cabinet ministers — and planning and dreaming. By late November more than 40 homes have been red-stickered, as well as some business premises. The town's rubbishman, Rob Roche, wants to avoid the track Christchurch took early on after 2011, where he says that demolishing and dumping outpaced recycling and conserving. Over the past 15 years his crews have diverted three-quarters of the town's waste from the tip, through composting, recycling and reusing. That figure, of 75 per cent by weight, is the best in New Zealand; Rob says that a crew in Raglan are right up there, too, hitting 75 per cent by volume — 'I think they might get us this year [by weight], but we'll do our best.'

Rob leads Innovative Waste Kaikōura, which runs the tip and the recycling shop and workshop, with its mini-gardens planted in old toilet bowls and its retro-cool old shop signs. He tells Kathryn Ryan on RNZ *Nine to Noon* that the town is talking, swapping ideas for sharing the load — even around such simple things as doing the Christmas shopping locally (though getting south or north to a mall might be tricky). 'We're rising up — we didn't expect we were going to rise 2 metres — but we're rising up and we'll be fine,' says Rob.

'We're very similar to 50-odd other community members around this country that really are making a difference in this space, and we're all about diversion of waste from landfill. We still have a landfill in this town, and potentially it could be in for a bit of a hit if we don't really come up with some good plans — zero waste is a kaupapa that this town stands on, and in my view always will … We see our landfill as a precious commodity that we're trying to protect, not an easy solution for waste.'

They're setting up what's called the Restoration Station, now just one month old, aimed at re-using the likes of rimu timbers from linings and balustrades from one of the pubs that needs to come down. Rekindle in Christchurch, which is already doing this, provides input. It is not about clearing it all away and starting from scratch on scorched earth: history gets protected, jobs get created, and things still get done by taking the longer way around. It can't come soon enough, though; Rob estimates that the quake's put paid to 100 or so jobs. 'We've got a real social vision as well as a waste vision … We've got a labour pool there for a wee while. I'm hoping the labour pool doesn't last actually, that they go back to their jobs; that'd be the ultimate. But in the meantime, short-term or medium-term, we've got a solution … With the local iwi, we've had initial chats with them and they're very keen to help out in terms of young rangitahi getting involved.'

> Not quite me own words but who cares. Kaikōura just wants good deconstruction outcomes & we're working to get there
>
> — @juliet_rekindle, tweet

Residual waste will eventually have to be carted out of town once the landfill is full. 'You know, recently we had a couple of buildings go out that were demolished before the quake, and they were just pulled down and trucked away, and we just don't want to see that if we can avoid it,' Rob tells Kathryn Ryan. 'Look at the opportunities — don't just look at putting it in a hole and covering it over, like Christchurch did in the early part. I understand they're revisiting some of those things now and regretting it. I think in the later part they had some really neat ideas, and we just want to pick from them … We can deconstruct these houses, we can reuse these materials and we can really make a difference in diversion.

'We've set this course many years ago … We've had a 7.8 shake — I don't see that stopping this kaupapa. I see it in some ways enhancing what we want to do, and maybe we're a template for others in the future, you know. [The way] I see it we've got to take it as an opportunity and prepare for it, if it ever happened again.'

———

The surfer and the seabed

'Just to let you all know this year's Surf Groms programme is kicking off a week late because we are waiting on new wetsuits from KBR. So we start November 12! We hope the water warms up a bit by then!'
— Kaikōura Surf Groms, Facebook, Oct 23

'We had family devastated after the Chch quakes
and we have been trying to think what we could do
to reach out to Kaikōura. We live just a few hundred
meters from the beach here … If you know any family
that wants/needs a break the cottage is available free
… Great surfing here in all directions.'

— Rosalie, a New Zealander living in Lombok, Indonesia,
on Facebook

Friday, December 2, 10.30am

Just north of the Hapuku River, the Meatworks surf break can be reached in 10 minutes from Kaikōura, particularly when you're racing against a flight departure time of noon, as we are, and when the main highway is all but deserted — even given that it has an awful lot of bumps and cracks and compacted-gravel repairs that weren't there before. We'd met Czech chef and surfer Filip Alobaid a short time earlier in the Coastal Sports shop. Surfboard salesman Rusty Boyd had been telling us how the Kahutara break just beyond the airport is possibly better now that the seabed is half a metre higher in South Bay. Rusty is working, so can't shoot out to the beach with us; he calls up Filip, who's free. The 29-year-old works later hours at The Whaler pub a little further along West End. Previously, he'd cooked alongside Jason Timms of Takahanga Marae at the now taped-off Adelphi Hotel.

Filip's keen to take us north to Meatworks. I've bought that $1 pair of dry trousers at the recycling centre and there's

90 minutes until our charter flight is due to leave. We tag along behind Filip and his German friend Louisa in their tired silver Toyota Estima, complete with surfboards and thick mattresses of uncovered foam in the back. A sharp turn just shy of a blind corner on the highway leads immediately to the beach, then to a rest area. We climb out and look west. Where I see a cold-looking sea, a grey-green wave curling up ominously to bash onto a beach consisting entirely of bone-breaking, bowling-ball-size boulders, and nothing between me and South America, Filip Alobaid sees a rhapsody. He's been surfing here for two or three years, and several times since the quake. 'We sleep in the van and I crack open my eye and look out at the sea, and if it's good to surf, that's a good day.'

So how has it changed at Meatworks? 'The low tide has definitely changed 'cos the ground has lifted ... See the distinctive rock over there?' Filip gestures to a glistening black rock intermittently being covered then exposed in the surf 20 metres off the beach. 'That's tapu, that's a sacred rock and ... it would be hidden under water on a high tide every time, but now that the ground has lifted you can see a lot more rocks exposed ... It's a bit more shallow, a bit more hollow which is more challenging for some ... The break has certainly changed its character, but it's still, it's still on, it's still good, it's still good surf.' He doesn't advise paddling out at Meatworks on a bigger day unless you are pretty good. He has hit the bottom already, and after his first ride on the remade waves needed stitches under his arm where his fin hit him. 'It could happen on a small day, on a big day,' he shrugs, then laughs and tells how a friend of theirs got bitten by a shark not long before. 'It was small one, maybe seven feet,' he says, miming a semi-circular bite mark from his knee to his backside. 'It got caught in his strap and panicked, and bit out,' says Louisa.

While we're on the subject of why *not* to go surfing, Louisa says she's hit her nose on the bottom — 'Yeah, I've got a little scar here … My new Christmas present, it would be really nice if it would be a helmet, you know, because you just feel safer … I tried to dive under the wave, and it pushed me down on the rocks so my face was just going down, on the rock … I came back up and couldn't feel my face and was like, "Ahh!" Tried to paddle to Fil to ask, "Hey, like, what do I look like? I can't feel my nose," and he was like, "Jesus Christ, you're getting out of the water now." Blood. It was a sunset session so he was like, "You're putting everyone else in danger," because there are sharks. He didn't really care too much about me, I think.'

Louisa's a bit of a grom — a beginner — but she trusts Filip. 'I wouldn't trust me,' he laughs. He adds that they need the right swell, at a good angle, to be able to judge exactly what's going on. 'There's certainly a couple of breaks in town that have improved and couple of breaks that might've gone worse.' Kahutara's benefited; Filip and Rusty agree on that.

They might not be so lucky at Mangamaunu just north of Meatworks. Filip and Louisa have paddled over. 'Because the whole earth lifted up for about 4 metres, so the point break wasn't working yet,' she says. 'Maybe with the right swell it might still be amazing, long waves into the bay — we are all hoping.' Could it be ruined? 'Might be,' she says. 'We are all hoping it's not, because it's like one of the best surf spots here.' Rusty Boyd back at the shop had seen it differently — that the break might now be twice as long, twice as good. I wonder, though, if this is a surfer thing, this surfeit of optimism; they all seem loath to diss a break.

Filip tucks his board under his arm, next to the stitches, and makes his way to the water, high-stepping over the boulders. Claire and I, though, are out of time. We get to the airport with 10 minutes to spare, but our pilot calls to say that the weather's keeping him in Christchurch for now. The waiting and reception area at Wings Over Whales beside the landing strip is peppered with people waiting like us. There's an edge of frustration mixed with agitation to get going — the polar opposite of the anticipation mixed with relaxation that until recently was the norm among holidaying tourists about to embark on a spot of whale-spotting.

A young American man is on his phone, informing distant friends that he's finally giving up on getting out and won't be seeing them after all. He carries his pack over to a small gold Yaris with an old couple in it and I hear him say, 'I'm Peter' — it appears that they've offered this stranger a lift back into town. When, at 3pm, we do eventually fly out, four of us cram into the Cessna with pilot Rupert. A couple has joined us; the man has his right arm in a sling and tells Rupert that he's broken his collarbone. He gets gingerly into the front seat. Oddly, before take-off he removes the sling, and biffs it back between Claire and me to his partner sitting in the rear cubbyhole. When we get out in Christchurch, he hefts his large bag over his right shoulder and off they both walk. I wonder whether we've just witnessed a medical ruse to get to the front of the exit line.

———

The kayaker and the cookbook

'The biggest part of it was the fact that no one has done it before.'
— Toby Johnstone, to RNZ, Dec 7

'Her mum, her aunt, her grandmother all crowded around proofreading and got it all sent off.'
— Genevieve King, to RNZ, Dec 9

Wednesday, December 7

Ben Judge at Clarence River Rafting is eyeing the river and wanting to get back into it. So, too, is his rafting guide Toby Johnstone. It's still too soon after the quake to launch the rafts, as there's too much they don't know about how the river has changed. Ben tells me he's aiming to get their first five-day trip in on the reconfigured river before Christmas, though that will depend on getting a Department of Conservation concession to drive along the Molesworth Station road to put their rafts in at Hanmer. DOC has been great, Ben says, and the river's not changed too much, going by what he has seen in low-level sweeps by plane — except, that is, in one spot within a stone's throw of their base a few kilometres from the river mouth and Toby Johnstone's cottage, right in the middle of the run where they take their half-day tours.

Here, the shifts in the Earth's crust have pushed a huge limestone slab up under what was a once gently flowing river that didn't drop very steeply. Now it does. The upraised rock has formed a giant step, with a channel being gouged down the middle of it by a rapid of at times frightening proportions. It was simply unrunnable directly after the quake. 'The thing is, it's just changing so much at the moment,' says Toby. 'Because it's fresh rock, when the earthquake happened it was in quite high flow, so boulders were rolling around and moving — so the nature of the rapid is changing very quickly.' He is keeping an eye on it, as the river eats back into the limestone — by up to 4 metres a day, by Ben's calculations. It changes from one day to the next, so just when he thinks it is good to go, 'I turn up the next day to run it and it's too gnarly, too dangerous, so I have got to wait until it changes again'. Toby must wait until the choice becomes less of a matter of cheating death.

At the rafting company's base, their admin person, Jacqui Hamilton, is also champing at the bit, but for a different reason. She can't get to her home up the valley because the Glen Alton bridge over the Clarence River fell down at 12.02am; and she can't get to her other job, two days a week down at a school in Hapuku, because the state highway is blocked. She has friends in the same boat, people who can't get to their jobs in a town that was once a 30-minute drive away. One works at the supermarket, another at the district council, and another drives a bus. Jacqui's home, along with seven or eight others, is to all intents and purposes cut off from anyone without a high-riding four-wheel-drive and nerves of steel. 'They have put in a temporary four-wheel-drive track up the south side through the Wharekiri and Miller streams and then through private property, so we can get in, but … you have to have a four–wheel-drive, you have to have a high-clearance vehicle, because the Wharekiri runs quite deeply, quite swift and scours out quite quickly. So for me I don't … at the moment I'm kind of stuck.'

Jacqui's neighbour, trophy-hunt operator Steve Millard, doesn't blame her for avoiding the road. He's bulldozed it, but the clay is slippery in the wet, and he's butted heads with the district council over putting gravel down. Jacqui asks him to sign her letter to the council protesting at how little information locals have had, both about the valley road and about State Highway 1 to Kaikōura, and about when — or even if — they'll be fixed. When every day new stories are appearing about the demolition of Wellington's buildings and the slip-clearing on the highway south of Kaikōura, it's just a little galling. Jacqui says it's ridiculous that she has to write a letter from inside an emergency zone to find out what's going on.

'So my issue, and those who live up the valley, is what's going to happen now? There's people who run businesses up there, there's a pine plantation that's going to need harvesting at some point, there's bed-and-breakfast, there's a game park, there's one of our local doctors lived there [Chris Henry] and then there was me, and I had a 10-acre block and I worked out part-time, and one of my neighbours worked out full-time, so it's a busy place.

'It's very sad and we're not getting very much information through about our situation, about how we're going to be able to reach our roads, how long it's going to take, what's the council doing about it ... There's been no conversations with the council. We haven't talked to the council at all since the earthquake ... I know the local MP was in our area 'cos he had a photo shoot in the local paper, but he certainly didn't come and speak with any of us up the Clarence Valley.'

Jacqui remains in good humour, though that won't stop her doing something about the matter. She'll send off the letter; maybe she'll even buy herself a four-wheel-drive. She laughs. Maybe that's not such an outlandish thought. The two sides of a coin flip and flip and flip again in the stories we are told: there are a lot of downsides, like Jacqui's, but then along comes an upside, like Toby's. The downsides can provide impetus: maybe Jacqui will look back on this as the time she got that high-riding four-wheel-drive that opened up the hinterland for her and steeled her nerves? Although the upsides are far fewer, they are all the more special for that: people seize on them, they lift their spirits.

The upside on the Clarence looks like this: a chute and a step and great volume of foaming water crashing down over it. 'We've been watching it for a while, the guides on the Clarence,' Toby tells RNZ's Guyon Espiner on December 7. 'I only looked at it yesterday and saw that it was runnable, and I couldn't help myself — I went home and got my kayak and ran it early this morning … yeah, went and did it.' He has pushed his bright green kayak into the grey-green water and hurtled down and over the step. 'Pretty amazing,' he says. 'I think the biggest part of it was the fact that no one has done it before, so that level of unknown … no one's ever done it. Pretty amazing feeling.'

It rates as a grade 3 rapid, on a scale of 1 to 5, he reckons. 'In the grand scheme of things you could find rapids like that in many other rivers,' says Toby, 'but it's quite a surprise to see it right in our backyard pop out of nowhere … Raft guides and kayakers, we are all quite excited about it, something good to come out of the earthquake.'

It's far from the only good thing. I caught up with Toby by phone the evening after his paddle. He's in St Arnaud with friend and fellow rafter Genevieve King, taking the long way round to

Christchurch to pick up the first book she's authored, a fresh-off-the-printing-press cookbook. Genevieve has matched local recipes with pictures and story-telling about some of the history of the rugged Clarence River valley. She almost didn't make this journey; almost didn't make it through with the book.

On the night of November 13 it was at the printer's, ready for proofing. Genevieve, though, was halfway up the Clarence towards Hanmer with a rafting group at Quail Flat. After the quake, her group was quickly choppered out — Genevieve to the lawn outside her parents Julia and Rick King's wrecked farmhouse.

The cottage Genevieve shares with Toby Johnstone is a wreck and will be red-stickered. 'To be honest, the book just completely went out of mind, it wasn't going to happen.' She laughs. 'There were far bigger fish to fry. The cottage had fallen down, and there was some pretty big issues at home with getting water to stock and all sorts. So yeah, the book was not important.' She laughs again.

Then her family stepped in, without her even knowing. 'So my brother's partner [Julia Macfarlane] was a little bit of a quiet lifesaver there. She's a graphic designer, and she quietly went ahead and called the printers, got the proofs, got her mum, her aunt, her grandmother all crowded around proofreading and got it all sent off.' They saw the value in a book that celebrated the Clarence pre-quake with pictures and some history, as well as recipes — 'with all the smiling locals holding up their lambs and showing off their lemon trees and all the rest of it … She wasn't going to let a little, or a rather large, earthquake stop it from happening just before Christmas. It had to happen.'

They have a plan to launch the cookbook at Sandy Bay on December 11. 'It's marking four weeks, a month on from the quake, and it will just be a great chance for everybody to come and see how we are all doing and have a hug,' says Genevieve. 'There's a large photo in the book of all the locals gathered on Boxing Day at Sandy Bay, and the sea's lapping against the rocks. And if you take a photo in that same spot now you have 200 metres of sandy beach out in front of you.' As it is, the weather's against them and the launch is held back at the family farm.

For Clarence locals, December 7 is quite a big day. Toby spends the morning making his own piece of history, in his wetsuit riding an infant rapid birthed by a geological spasm — and how many can say they've ever done that? — and the evening heading off with Genevieve to pick up her own piece of history made with a measuring spoon and a camera. The new and the old book-ended in a single day.

The cookbook, *Valley Gatherings*, has become a bit more than it was; it's now a marker between quake and pre-quake, a small signpost in time. It sits between the Clarence that was, providing a glimpse of that physical place in among the lists of ingredients for lemon cake and damper, and the Clarence that now is, reworked by a seismic shudder. You can see such markers in a lot of places now: the limestone slab in the river; the slip taking the troublesome overhang off a cliff above State Highway 1; the new dive spots, Lake Rebekah, the trenches ploughshared through farmland and lifestyle blocks, shallower surf breaks above repopulating pāua and crayfish beds. Further afield, Wellington's wharf won't be the same. Hanmer and Culverden and Seddon and Ward are all changed, a little or a lot.

Genevieve King has just enough time before her cookbook goes to print to slip in a little paragraph in the front. 'It says,' she tells me, '"At the time this book was going to print our world was turned upside down ... As I sit writing this perched on a new bank about 20 metres higher than it was last week, looking out over newly sculpted paddocks to a new grade 5 rapid in the Clarence River, I get the feeling there are a few more stories to be shared from this beautiful valley and its incredibly resilient people. Let's just call this a prequel, shall we?"'

———

Good news

'Someone told us we were the first tourists to use it, and we were like "Oh?"'
— Coral, to RNZ, Dec 19

RNZ's Max Towle finds Kaikōura eerily quiet in mid-December. The emergency service workers might not all have gone, but there are far fewer of them about. Outside the Why Not Café, appropriately, Max comes across a couple of tourists, Coral and Kim from the UK, who drove up the Inland Road on its first day of regular use. 'We didn't even know the road was closed, and someone told us we were the first tourists to use it, and we were like, "Oh?"' says Coral. 'It took us ages to get here, and even when we rolled into town our petrol tank was on red,' says Kim. 'We literally rolled into town.'

The town may be quiet, but they are still impressed. 'It looks beautiful and the weather is great — we were just on the West Coast and it was a bit cold and wet … Just the colour of the water here, we've never seen anything like it,' Kim tells Max.

Colette Cargill, who runs clothing and knick-knack shop Little Rock, feels the pressure lifting a little, helped on its way by a surprise visitor. 'I had a lady come in who had driven all the way up from Christchurch just to do some shopping in Kaikōura, which was magic … It's amazing, and all they have to do now is get the marina going and Kaikōura will be back on its feet.'

'… tourists are returning for the first time since last month's quakes. After five weeks of the town being cut off, the Inland Road finally opened today to traffic in both directions, and businesses say with summer holidays fast approaching, it will bring a welcome boost to the local economy. Daniel Jenkins … told me businesses had already noticed a difference.'
— John Campbell, on RNZ *Checkpoint*, Dec 19

Afterword

'We're due for a big one [in Portland], so this one kind
of gave us an idea.'

— an Oregon tourist, to John Key, in Kaikōura , Nov 16

It seems to me that earthquakes are the least forgiving of
disasters. They strike us at home or at work, and everywhere in
between. They are all around us. You can shelter from a cyclone
or flee a fire, but the only immunity from a quake is not to be
there in the first place. But here we are, God help us. I shake my
head sometimes and wonder why I haven't packed up my family
and taken the children somewhere it doesn't shake so much, like
Brisbane, or England, or Auckland even.

The tourists in Kaikōura responded to the 7.8 in the only way
that makes any kind of sense: they rushed to get the hell out,
away from the aftershocks. The locals, too, scarpered where
they could. But they have gone back and, by and large — in the

same way as after the Canterbury 2011 quake — they mean to stay. Lodge owner Jenny Yeoman is implacable about that. Trish Mulvaney is, too. In Wellington, no one I know has suddenly upped sticks for Tauranga, though plenty have for the first time taken the time to seriously nut out an evacuation plan and pack a decent go-bag.

So, if we are not going anywhere, then we need to get our buildings right. There is plenty of work going on to achieve that. However, there are also plenty of signs that we are not doing enough. For much of 2016 before the November quake, I worked for RNZ on stories about the construction industry; in particular, structural steel and seismic reinforcing mesh. These stories demonstrated that this country has much looser policing of the standards that are meant to apply to building product quality than Europe, Australia and the United States. Substandard products can be allowed in, and these get built into our homes, offices, roads and waterworks. It's time to go back to the evidence and findings of the Canterbury Earthquakes Royal Commission, and the technical investigation into why the CTV and other buildings collapsed, and check whether we followed through.

In November, the Christchurch City Council confirmed that it was investigating claims of sub-standard welding work on five buildings. Would anyone really want to take chances five years on as part of that city's rebuild? In Wellington, the central business district was declared open 32 hours after the Kaikōura quake. A month later, engineers found that the bolts holding heavy concrete panels onto the façade of a central city bank were broken. They were at risk of falling off into the street in an aftershock. The building was quickly evacuated and fixed. A little over 24 hours, said the council's building control manager Mike Scott, and 'it will be back to business as usual'.

Business as usual? Let's hope not. Have the bolts been tested? Let's hope so. I think the tourist from Oregon who shook John Key's hand in the park at Kaikōura and told him she'd learned something about what Portland might face, and what it should do, was closer to where we want to be at. It's only fatalistic to stay put if we don't build — and rebuild — better.

Phil Pennington
Wellington
December 2016

Acknowledgements

The production of this book has relied on three things: people sharing their stories, teamwork, and Bob Dronfield lending us his ute when we first got to Kaikōura.

The team at HarperCollins had the idea to take some of the reportage on the earthquake and put it in book form. Thanks especially to Alex Hedley for shepherding this through to completion.

The team at Radio New Zealand were there and reported the stories, and, without that, this project would have gone nowhere. Thanks to Paul Thompson and Carol Hirschfield for appreciating the opportunity provided here to retell those stories; thanks to our news directors Mary Wilson, Brent Edwards and Alex van Wel, executive editors Martin Gibson and Pip Keane, and the producers whose hard work under high pressure allowed the public to hear about and see what was going on in the first place;

thanks to RNZ's technical people who surmount obstacle after obstacle to get the news to the public, in particular to Simon Dickinson for his unfailing patience in sorting out the glitches; and thanks to the reporters and video journalists whose work is compiled and pictured here, in particular Conan Young, Tim Graham, Rebekah Parsons-King, Claire Eastham-Farrelly, Tracy Neal, Alex Perrottet, Simon Morton, Kate Newton, Ian Telfer, Sally Murphy, Eva Corlett, Max Towle, Patrick O'Meara and Chris Bramwell.

The biggest thanks goes to the people in these pages, those from Kaikōura, Waiau, Mt Lyford, Ward, Clarence, Kēkerengū, Oaro and Wellington, who took the time under stress and duress to talk to me and the other reporters in the field. Thanks, too, to the dozens of tourists from all over the planet we spoke to, having a holiday they will never forget. These people were almost all gracious and good-humoured, and only swore at the occasional aftershock (mostly). Bob Dronfield exemplified that spirit: without his ute we could not have covered many of the stories told here. Thanks.

A Message from New Zealand
Red Cross

Supporting Kiwis through tough times

It was clear this was a big one. The 7.8 magnitude earthquake that hit in the early hours of 14 November was one of the strongest earthquakes ever felt in New Zealand, sending shockwaves right across the country. New Zealand Red Cross Disaster Welfare and Support Teams were quickly deployed to the worst-hit areas in Marlborough and Kaikōura. Here, the quake and its aftershocks blocked roads, destroyed buildings and ripped apart the land.

One of the teams' first tasks was setting up Civil Defence Centres for people unable to return to damaged homes. The centres not only offered people a safe place to sleep, they also provided access to food and water, information and emotional support. People need food, water and a bed, but just as important is having someone there for a bit of support. Not knowing if you'll have a home to go back to, or when an aftershock will hit, can be extremely stressful, but sometimes a friendly chat can help.

Red Cross volunteers also helped Civil Defence and the New Zealand Army evacuate tourists stranded in Kaikōura after the quake. About 1000 tourists were flown to Christchurch by helicopter, where they were met by Red Cross volunteers.

Red Cross Kaikōura Branch President Lorraine Diver and other local members spent long hours putting together food parcels, bottled water and essential supplies to deliver to people throughout the district.

With roads damaged and supplies running short in the town, the parcels were a helping hand for families like Shannen, Justin and their toddler, Zaiden, after the quake. Red Cross dropped into the family's rural home near Kaikōura to deliver a care parcel and check the three were okay. Shannen told team members she had been afraid to go into the house — even though it was declared safe — and they had spent several nights sleeping in the car.

'It's just nice to see a friendly face,' she said. 'I've been a bit scared for Zaiden and I have no family in the South Island. And this food will definitely help. He loves fruit!'

The physical damage caused by the earthquake is easy to see. Less visible, but just as powerful, are the psychological impacts